I0553485

94 Creations 7

Publisher
Adriena Dame

Co-Managing Editors
Amy Jackson
Angela Jackson-Brown

Editors
Charlene Luck
Carmen Brown
Patti Charron
Elizabeth Filiatreau
Nuray Yasayanlar

94 Creations is a literary journal committed to celebrating previously unpublished fiction, creative nonfiction, drama, poetry, art, and whatnot.

94 Creations
www.94creations.com

978-0-9857056-9-5

94 Creations 7

PUBLISHER'S NOTE

94 Creations is a print literary journal committed to publishing an eclectic assortment of outstanding fiction, creative nonfiction, poetry, drama, and art by both emerging and established writers and artists. We welcome the gritty, offbeat, marvelous works often overlooked in mainstream publishing venues, as well as those works that create an authentic experience within the framework of more conventional literary landscapes. We are also interested in celebrating diversity, and are eager to attract the attention of exceptional writers of diverse backgrounds.

Narvelle Jasmine Alexander Littleton (1913-2007), my grandmother, was a significant inspiring force behind the founding of this publication. Despite the hardships of raising nine children in rural Arkansas during a time when racism and sexism prevailed, she found countless ways to exercise her creativity, and to thrive as an artist. I am proud to be a part of the legacy she helped to forge.

I am also thankful for our volunteer editorial team, a group of quirky, kick-ass women who make the journal happen amidst their busy schedules. It is always my hope that our individual and collective efforts continue to be driven by the love affair we have with the written word.

I am especially grateful for our co-managing editors, Amy Jackson and Angela Jackson-Brown, who continue to do an exemplary job of leading the team through the editorial process, even when the road gets rocky.

May those of you who are avid readers, read on. May those of you who are writers, write on. May those of you who simply want to support a quality publication, support on. I am sure that I can speak for the entire *94 Creations* editorial team when I say, you matter to us.

Warm regards,

Adriena Dame

EDITORIAL TEAM

PUBLISHER

Adriena Dame, author of *The Moo: Stories and a Novella* and publisher of *Iris Brown Lit Mag*, is a professor of undergraduate creative writing courses at Spalding University, and a board member for Louisville Literary Arts, Kentucky Foundation for Women, and Generation iSpeak. She also designs SOSAJI! Socks and Damejoyas jewelry art, and teaches English as a Second Language.

CO-MANAGING EDITORS

Amy Jackson is a fiction writer who grew up in southeastern Kentucky and wandered around Providence, Rhode Island and San Francisco before finally heeding the call to come back to the South. She has an MA in English

 from the University of Kentucky and wrote her thesis on Lewis Carroll and the relationship between writer and reader. Amy currently lives in Louisville, Kentucky with her dog Lucky and is working on her first novel.

Angela Jackson-Brown is the author of *Drinking From a Bitter Cup*, published in 2014 by WiDo Press, is a poet and writer residing in Indianapolis, Indiana. She is an English professor at Ball State University and a graduate of the

Spalding University's low-residency MFA in Writing Program. Her work appears in *Pet Milk, The Louisville*  *Review, New Southerner Literary Magazine, 94 Creations* and *Muscadine Lines: A Southern Journal.* Her short story, "Something in the Wash," was awarded the 2009 fiction prize by *New Southerner Literary Magazine* and was nominated for a Pushcart Prize in Fiction.

EDITORS

Charlene Luck is a fiction writer from the Greater Detroit Area. She is a graduate of the University of Michigan's MFA in prose program, where she completed her thesis, a collection of short stories titled "In Your Houses." Her short story, "Grey Herons," was a finalist in the Glimmer Train Stories Summer Short-Short Fiction Contest 2007. She lives in Louisville, Kentucky with her husband, Jeff, and three cats: Manny, Mike, and Cheszwyck.

Nuray Yasayanlar is from the old stomping ground of Homer, Izmir, Tŭrkiye and lives in Louisville, Kentucky. She graduated from Hacettepe University's English Language and Literature Department and earned an MA in Teaching from Spalding University. While she most enjoys writing poetry and creative non-fiction, her writing life began with journalistic flair during her high school years;

she would pen editorials in her blue, leather-covered journals after watching the evening news. Her fellowship with Louisville Writing Project fired her creative passion, and her participation in Mixed Nuts Writers Group continues to fuel her commitment to writing. Currently, she teaches English at Central High School.

Elizabeth Filiatreau has had a hand in grant writing, newspaper editing, and publishing as a guest columnist in the Courier-Journal. After years of following other people's dreams, she is in pursuit of her own brand of happiness, which includes becoming a successful writer. She has two children and two grandchildren, and she lives in Kentucky with her dog Zoey Doodle, who only interrupts her writing when it interferes with her suppertime.

Carmen Moreno-Rivera is a Kentucky-born AfroLatina hellbent on changing the world one word at a time.

Patti Charron is a writer and editor based in Louisville, Kentucky. Dangling modifiers get on her nerves.

CONTENTS

TOM KELLY loves brunch as much as the next jaded millennial. He is an MFA candidate at Old Dominion University in Norfolk, Virginia. His poems and editorials have appeared, or are forthcoming, in *FreezeRay*, *Utter Foolery: The Best Global Literary Humor 2015*, and *Four Ties Lit Review*.

Tourist in Planet Your

For Miley Cyrus

Seven minutes until show time I shrink
to a barely visible crumb and tuck myself
onto a peppermint beneath your tongue.
I ride through your nervous mouth, sailing
in a sea of lukewarm saliva, soak
my hair in the mist, let your hot breath beat
my face like northeasterly breezes.
I feel the tumult of your tongue rock
my body and the foundation on which I stand.
Suddenly I plummet, drop down the chute
of your throat. I tour the tautness of your larynx,
your tired trachea, warming itself awake.
I dive into the depths of your diaphragm and
esophagus, wondering how long it will take
to reach the ecosystem of your gut.
Is it winter or summer in your stomach
when I arrive? The pink-lined sky
rains torrents of gastric acid. Nestled deep,
I burn into a million pieces, disintegrate
like a dying star—explode into every part
of your body. Parts of me pump into your veins,
do backstrokes in your bloodstream, experience
the tension in your tendons as you dance.
Other parts scatter into the synapses
of your brain—shatter upon contact
with neurons coming my way. But the better parts
are lost in the chambers of your heart—absorbing

the pace of its beat and pulse: quick but steady
like a hummingbird's wings: tireless slave
working to remain fixed in the same place.

When Loving a Mouse Becomes Too Hard

After Gary Jackson

Over a few lines of blow, Minnie rants that she occasionally makes Mickey do the *he-hup*, *golly*, and whistle while they fuck because she gets off on pretending that Mickey's just as charming and vivacious as the mouse he plays in the movies. Daisy can't empathize because she's only done the dirty with Disney's Donald Duck: the same feathered freak that everyone sees on the big screen: absolutely quack in the sack, bar none the best domestic male she's ever tangoed tails with. Minnie says that lately she's been curious about Donald and envies the idea of sleeping with one mouse: inseparable from his public persona. What does it matter if Mickey's hung like a hamster, when he's too hung over to make a mouse in heat moan? Most of the time, he just flops around meeker than a mole above ground. But once in a blue cheese, she concedes, it's *Fantasia* complete with floating furniture and fireworks. The way he shouts *God bless!* and *Oh boy!* mid-hump-n-pump morphs their mattress into something like the Magic Kingdom. Daisy chimes in that both their boyfriends are wild, sexy animals even if they're different breeds. But Minnie broods on the image of Mickey stuffing his fat fur into his red, button fly shorts in their bedroom before work, the familiar pre-nine-to-five frown pinning his lips and cheeks in place, while she hangs on the bed's edge —hoping that he'll have one of his happy-horny-furball, scurry into the sheets and rodent around moments, shout *pa-ha! Mouse me, Minnie!* then proceed to talk Mickey as shit to her—just before he heads out the door and turns into the mouse she longs for, a mouse that belongs to Walt Disney. Most mornings she doesn't even see him break into a smile. But she clings to the possibility like a fleeting tail.

LINA PATTON is currently working on her MFA at George Mason University, where she is Assistant Fiction Editor of the literary journal, *Phoebe* and teaches English Lit. She is the 2015 recipient of George Mason's Thesis Fellowship in Fiction and has work pending in *Five Quarterly*.

We Will Spark

Maria and I are stretched across two lounge chairs at the hotel pool. The plastic strips are hot and press and curve into our thin, wet bodies when we sit down. Maria has on my pink and red bikini because she's not allowed to own things so revealing, and when she lifts her arm to wipe the sweat from her top lip, I see her whole body lying there, and think how much better the bikini looks on her. Next to us, there are men with curling gray chest hair playing cards and drinking from little plastic cups full of dark liquid and limes. Their ice cubes disappear in the heat faster than the drops of pool water on my stomach, and they keep waving to the waitress for more. Behind them are a mother and father rubbing sunscreen into the small, plump arms of their baby daughter, and beyond them are more half-naked bodies I watch from behind my sunglasses, staring at the women, comparing their bodies and chests to my own. Everyone is out today, I think. And why wouldn't they be, with the 97 degree weather and large kidney pool sparkling cleaner than it is, with the tall, sloping palm trees placed strategically for shade.

Maria and I came to Las Vegas with my mom, who came on business. We are both fourteen and it is July, and in the next two days my mother will be busier than she expected, we will have more time to ourselves than we first thought. After our first day at the pool, we will weave through the hotel casino and spend twenty minutes looking for the elevator to the seventeenth floor. We will be barefoot and laugh at how confused we are, pull our sunglasses down when we pass the same blackjack table three times and the Asian woman in the yellow jacket stares at us again.

We will find the elevator and spend the rest of the afternoon admiring our tan lines and the photos I took at the pool. I will delete most of the pictures that are not of Maria—the palm trees and fountains spitting water overexposed in the bright sun—but will be pleased that some shots look artistic, like Maria is a model in some far off location. She will still claim that she looks bad, but she will not tell me to delete them.

When I finish checking the photos and making sure no water has crept into the crevices of my camera, a Nikon D5000 my mother gave me for my birthday, we will go into the bathroom and peel off our sundresses, wring out our hair. We will stand together in front of the mirror and pull the triangles of our swimsuits aside, exposing the line from pale, smooth skin to skin that is red and hot. Maria will be tanner than me, have a harsher line across the side of her small breast, and I will be jealous. I will tell her I wish I had her tan, but really I will wish I had her whole body: her slender knees, the way her torso curves on either side like the inner slopes of crescent moons, her straight pretty nose. We will change into sweatpants and the blue t-shirts from our basketball team. Then we will lie on the same bed watching reruns of *Friends* until my mom calls and tells us to order room service for dinner, that she will be later than she thought.

When it gets dark and the lights from the strip spark up our window, we will become restless and feel like we should be doing something since we are in Las Vegas and want something to tell our friends. We will put on miniskirts, folding their waistbands to make them shorter, bare more flesh, and go down to the hotel lobby. Maria will wear a pair of my mom's heels even though I ask her not to, partly because they are my mom's, and partly because her legs look so long. We will reach the main floor and sit on one of the marble benches and watch people walk by. Maria will sigh, and I will worry this trip will not be as fun as I had made it sound. Then a man checking into the hotel will stare at Maria. She will nudge me and smile back at him, dip her head to the side and let her hair feather along her cheek. He will wave, his elbows still resting on the counter. She will turn to me and laugh, and I'll laugh because she is and because somehow it is exciting, and I will hope the man does not look away too soon.

We will spend the rest of the night strutting through the two hotels connected to our own and catching the eyes of strangers. After the first group of boys whistles at us on the escalator, I will call my mom and tell her we are out taking pictures of all the neon lights, and she will say okay, to stay together and not walk more than a few hotels away, that she will be home late. I will tell Maria my mother doesn't care at all, that we can do whatever we want, but I should still probably take some pictures to make sure she believes us. Maria will say great and then link arms with me. We will push through the hotel's revolving doors and head toward the walkway that passes up and over traffic. We will climb the stairs together and head across the strip, the cars and taxis and streams of headlights all moving fast below us.

We will continue walking through new lobbies and casinos and will be surprised by the attention we receive, will soak it in and laugh when men swivel in their stools to watch us as we pass, their hands still on the levers of their singing slot machines. I will pause once in a while to take a photo of a ceiling painted in bright colors or a line of limos by an entrance, but we will move quickly to cover more ground, steal more looks.

We will not stop to talk to anyone until two men from a bachelor party come up to us by the water fountain. When they approach us, Maria will be fixing the back strap of her sandal, leaning with her shoulder against the wall as she bends her knee to bring her heel closer, and I will be taking a drink, enjoying the smooth cool water that reminds me of the pool. They will startle us both when they say, hey girls, will cause Maria to stomp her foot down to regain balance. But we will straighten and look at each other, Maria will touch the ends of her hair and say hello in the voice I know she uses on the phone and when she talks to teachers, and they will both tell us we look gorgeous.

They will be dressed in dark gray suits and look like they are thirty, tell us they are here for a friend's bachelor party and got separated from the group. Maria will do most of the talking and introduce us both, say that we are on our way out for the night. The one with the dark eyebrows and undershirt that looks too small will keep his eyes on me, ask me directly if I like Las Vegas and if I've been here before. I will look to Maria and then answer him, tell him that I haven't. He will keep looking at me, stare at the necklace resting against the high flat bone of my chest, and tell me I look stunning. I will comb my hair behind my ears and Maria will ask them where they're going, but then a group of men will come walking toward us, their slick shoes loud against the marbled tile, and they will shake their heads and laugh, yell to their friends to come back and leave us alone.

We will talk to a few more people the rest of the night: boys from Nebraska playing in a basketball tournament, a man who says he dresses up as Elvis on Thursdays, a group that asks us to play craps. But we will not spend too long with any of them, and Maria will carry the conversations, although I will pay close attention to each word, look for a place to add something of worth. Still, we will not talk for long. We will take their compliments and leave, Maria squeezing my hand hard when she has had enough. And when her feet start to hurt after another hour, we will be tired and go back to our hotel. We will climb into bed carefully and whisper goodnight, now feeling closer to each other after the night we had, and I will fall asleep replaying everything in my mind, seeing all the images and feeling happy someone called me beautiful, even if it isn't true.

The next day we will sleep late, then go back to the pool. Two older women will be in our chairs from the day before, so we will walk to the opposite side, the concrete hot and stinging. We will talk about the night before, Maria laughing with her eyes closed as we imitate the pick-up lines and the ways guys stared. It will be hotter than the day before, and we will get in the water and stay in until our fingertips prune into ridges and our hair is slick and smelling of chlorine. In the pool, we will judge each other's handstands, and she will rate mine better.

We will eat lunch with my mom and both order cheeseburgers. My mom will order wine and salad and ask to see my pictures from the night before. I will be embarrassed by the photos, will know they all look rushed and forced, but I will still pass her my camera and she will still tell me they look lovely. I will worry there will be some pictures that give our night away—a flash of a suit jacket or Maria's back turned to a guy—but I will know that I was careful, and that even if there were those types of pictures, my mother never looks too closely.

After lunch she will go back to our room to finish work, and Maria and I will continue working on our tans. Just when we are about to leave, feeling too hot and too tired, a boy with big broad shoulders and a red swimsuit will sit sideways on the chair beside us. He will introduce himself as Jake, and will have short blonde hair that bristles over the tops of his ears and a tattoo on his right collarbone of a word I cannot read. He will point behind him to a group of guys who will all wave back. He will say they just arrived, are trying to make friends, and would like for us to join them. Maria will look at me quickly, tighten the strings of her suit tied behind her neck, and say that we would love to.

We will grab our towels, bags, and scoot on our flip flops before we follow Jake. I will look at the group of guys, all young and tanned and strong, and will touch Maria's arm and whisper I do not want to be there long. She will nod and say okay, but I will not be sure she really hears me, so I will repeat myself again. She will roll her eyes, pull her beach bag higher on her shoulder and say I know, loud enough that it will make Jake turn around.

We will lay our towels beside their chairs and sit as they shake our hands. I will watch their muscles flex and tighten my own abs, wipe the sweat from behind my knees with the backs of my wrists and wonder how I look to them. One of the five guys will drag a blue cooler from underneath a lounge chair, say they brought their own refreshments since the place is such a rip-off. He will pop the tops of cool, sweating beers and pour each into cups they brought. The sun will move out from behind a cloud, and we will all start squinting. Maria and I will be handed our own full cups even though we did not ask for them. We will look at each other, smile quietly, and I will know we are both thinking about retelling this to Becky and Louise at school. Then the boys will raise their glasses to us, and Maria, then I, will take a small and bitter sip.

We will spend almost two hours with Jake and his friends, although we will mostly talk to Jake and one other guy named Matt. We will learn they are college seniors from Arizona State and are here to celebrate a birthday. Maria will tell them we are starting college this year and I will nod along. We will tell them we are here with my older sister, and when Matt asks me if she is hot, I will say that I don't know. Maria will say of course, that she looks like an older version of myself, and Matt will say that's good. I will blush and be thankful for the sunburn that is already spread across my cheeks. Then we will swim and talk some more and drink one and a half beers. We will agree to meet them later by the bar in our hotel's casino. Jake will give Maria his number, type it into her phone himself and fold it back into her hand. We will say goodbye and leave, wait until we are through the hotel doors to grab each other's elbows and laugh and let our voices overlap. We will ask if we feel drunk, both agree we think we might, and move loudly through the hallways to our room, our thoughts and excitement and the sharp cold air conditioning pulling up the goose bumps along our moving limbs.

That night, we will try on seven different outfits and wear eyeliner twice as thick as normal. My mother will be at a dinner and award ceremony and will say again, she won't be home till late. But when we start picking out our outfits, before she leaves, she will ask why we are dressing up. Before I can respond, Maria will tell her we're going to do a photo shoot, that we're going to take turns walking an imaginary catwalk down the hotel lobbies, that my photos will look professional. My mother will agree they will be nice, like fashion editorials, but will tell us to be careful. She will say to take some by the famous fountain, to go see the water show that plays each night. I will agree, and before she steps out the door, she will kiss me on the forehead and tell us to be good. I will feel guilty about lying to her, but decide that it could be the truth: I really will spend the night taking pictures I can show her. I will become excited as I think about it, that I could maybe even take some great ones to use at my photo camp next month.

We will finish getting ready sitting cross-legged on the bathroom counter, our faces inches from the mirror, fogging it up with our breath as we lean close to curl our lashes. Maria will kiss the small circle of condensation when she is done, her lips leaving a mark like a small petal ripped in half. When our makeup is set, we will straighten our hair using the flat iron Maria brought. I will burn the side of my cheek slightly when I attempt to smooth my bangs, but Maria will get me a cold washcloth and help me finish, all the time telling me how much Matt liked me. I will look at her in the mirror as her hands work through my hair and tell her how much Jake stared at her, how pretty he must have thought she was. But she will say no, that he was looking at some other girls more, and I will not argue with her. When we are done, we will look in the full-length mirror one last time, snap a few pictures of each other posing in our outfits, then go down to the casino. Maria will be wearing a black dress she wore to our friend's birthday party with sequins on the straps. I will be wearing a dark teal tank top that is too small and the same skirt from the night before. We will think we look older, maybe even sexy.

When we get to the bar, Jake will not be there. We will sit on stools at one far side out of sight of the bartender. We will force ourselves to talk about our friends from school and getting our driving permits, pretend that we aren't anxious. I will take some pictures of Maria and some older women with drinks in tall colorful glasses, but Maria will tell me to put my camera back in my purse, that they will be here soon and we need to act mature. She will check her phone and pick at the sequins of her dress, three will come unthreaded and she will drop them on the floor. After twenty minutes, we will see Jake walking toward us. He will be with Matt, another guy from the pool, and four more we will not recognize. His buttoned shirt will be untucked and stained. He will yell, Maria, then sling his heavy arms around us. He will smell like alcohol, although I will not know which kind. Still, he will be funny, and Matt will touch my knee.

We will spend a while sitting together drinking the syrupy sweet drinks Matt brings back clutched between his hands and knuckles, which will taste good, and better than the beer. Maria and I will tap each other with our toes beneath the stools and laugh at everything they say. I will think how we must look to others, how jealous I would be if I were walking past on the maroon paths of the casino carpet and spotted a group of older girls and guys drinking and leaning up against each other. I will smile and wish I could take a picture.

But soon the bartender will walk toward us behind the granite sloping countertop and stop. He will look at us and ask for our IDs, holding out his hand with fingers two inches apart, pinching an imaginary license like a solid piece of air. The boys will shuffle for their wallets and I will duck into my purse, finger the same folds over and over again, feel the sweat beneath my arms bleed into the fabric of my top. Maria will tell him—them—that we forgot ours in the room. Jake will laugh when the bartender takes our drinks, push Maria's hair from the front to the back of her shoulder, letting his hand brush against her chest as he pulls it away, and say he forgot we were only freshmen. Then he will say we should just get some more drinks from his room. Matt and the others will say they want to play poker. They will say they'll meet us soon and disappear through the blinking sounds and lights.

Jake, Maria and I will ride the elevator to the twenty-third floor. I will look at Maria through the elevator mirror and will know we are both ignoring thoughts about my mother, about lines that have been drawn for us. But Jake will start singing, we will recognize the words, and will follow him down the long, bright hallways when the elevator doors chime open. We will get to room 2319 and he will unlock the door. We will go inside and smile when we see the room, realize it's a suite. We will recognize some decorations, the same picture of the ocean and spikey green plants as our room, but we will be impressed by all the extra doors and hallways, the kitchen and white leather couches making it look like something from a magazine. Maria will say, wow, and he will say he knows, but this is just his style.

Maria will sit on top of one of the slick black kitchen counters and begin to swing her legs, the clinking of her heels like the quiet pulsing of a clock. Jake will come up beside her and put one hand on top of her thigh, but will pull it away as he turns to me, then will ask if we like vodka. Maria will say yes and I will agree. He will pull a clear blue bottle, half empty, from the freezer and set it on the counter, open up the cabinets to grab glasses, then see they are empty and rinse two from the sink. After pouring an inch of liquid and dropping some ice cubes into each, he will hand them to us. He will take a swig from the bottle and go to turn on the stereo in the corner of the room, snap his fingers along to the music he has not yet started playing.

Maria will look at me and smile, then shrug and take a sip. She will twist her face and cough into the back of her hand, but it will give her courage, and she will get off the counter and start to look around. Holy crap, she will say, pulling the white curtains back from the window, telling me to come look at the view. I will come up beside her and tell her that it's beautiful, because it really will be, and lean closer into her so I can see farther to the left, making our shoulders touch. We will stand together for a minute, both admiring how the window isn't facing the strip, but rather the mountains and houses moving away from Las Vegas, their roofs small and flat and glowing from the moon that is just starting to press into view. I will turn to look at her after tracing my eyes through the details of outside, will notice how the purpling blue sky of the early night illuminates her face, makes her skin look soft, and I will tell her I want to take a picture. She will say fine, but then turn and say she wants to keep exploring.

Jake will get the stereo working and start singing more loudly. He will take another large swig from the bottle he is holding and will stand up on the couch, his shirt coming more and more undone. He will bounce up and down and start to tell us how much he loves this city. He will grab Maria's thin wrist and pull her up to him. She will step up beside him, but lose her balance quickly, unsteady from her heels digging into the couch cushions, which will make Jake grab her closer, press their bodies tight together. I will watch them both sway back and forth, will know they are about to fall, but then will watch Jake kiss her. He will have his hand on the back of her head, holding his mouth hard against hers. She will pull back, laugh, her face hot and flushed, then give him a small hug and step down from the couch.

I will look at Maria, pick up my purse, but she will only glance at me before turning back to the kitchen. She will grab her drink and take a sip as she walks back toward us, her eyes still avoiding mine, then will set her glass on the low coffee table and say she's not done looking around. She will add she'll be right back, to keep on drinking, will start walking down a hallway. I will watch her check herself in the mirror as she goes, smoothing out her dress and readjusting the bottom wires of her bra before she disappears into a different room.

I will take a sip of my own drink and stare down the hallway, will try to ignore the unease pounding with my heart. Jake will get up and go into the kitchen, fill a glass higher than he did for either of ours and finish it in one long sip while leaning back against the fridge. I will turn and keep looking out the window, will try to pretend I am somewhere else, then start to focus on everything outside: the way the moon becomes more visible as the sky climbs to a darker shade of blue, how the lights from all the houses start to look like scattered stars across the ground. Holding my drink in my left hand, I will dig into my purse with the other, my fingers searching for the familiar case of my camera. I will find it and pull it out, take a breath. I will try to focus it through the window, but the lights from the room will glare sharply off the glass, reflect back the couch and tables and a rough image of Jake in the kitchen, and I will look for a different angle. Then I will notice a small balcony to my side. I will look back down the hallway, see Maria's legs move into another room, see Jake now sitting at the counter, and will decide to step outside.

I will tuck my camera underneath my arm and unlock the polished gold latches and knobs of the door, move out onto the small, white balcony. The wind will be stronger than I expected, but I will like the way it feels moving underneath my shirt, the air clean and cool. I will set my drink down on the balcony deck and use both hands to steady my camera, balance my elbows on the railing so my pictures won't be shaky. I'll take several at a time, carefully framing the spread of houses and palm trees that disappear in the distance, the mountain peaks and moon making them all look smaller. I will start to feel these will be the best pictures I have ever taken, the balcony propelling me closer to my image of the sky while letting me look down on everyone's neatly placed homes, their still windows burning with artificial, sparkling light.

After my last few clicks, I will scan back through my pictures, my thumb repeatedly pushing the arrow left, and will smile to myself as the images roll across the screen. I will feel relaxed from my photos and the cool air around me, and will decide Maria would want to see the balcony, too. I will call her name and look through the glass door, but will keep scanning through the photos, only turning it off when I reach the ones from earlier that night, an image of Maria posing in our room—her hands on her hips and head back laughing—appearing just as the screen goes blank. I will call her name again and keep looking through the door, but will not be able to see too far inside, so I will go to the balcony edge and lean over the railing, try to see into the windows farther down the wall while the wind pulls my hair across my eyes and face. I will think I can see the hallway, will think I can see one of the doors slammed shut, and I will straighten up quickly, step back, then pull open the balcony door and go inside. I will call her name again, move toward the hallway, but pause once I am standing in the middle of the living room and notice how it is now louder and empty, Maria's glass still full and resting on the table, the stereo turned up.

CATHARINE BATSIOS is from Flint, MI, and is an alumnus of Michigan State University. She currently lives in Detroit, where she is the Creative Writing Intern for 826michigan. She writes in most of her spare time and workshops regularly on Sundays with her comrades, the Daedalus Poets.

Ode to Leaves Growing into the Window, July 2007
or
With all these Leaves, I Finally Figured You Out

It was the summer of 113½ Louis Street—

Summer of unsent letters to my friend who left to
study in Mexico, summer of crawling through the
window and shrubs to work at the gas station on the
other side, summer

of duct-taping blue scarves on the ceiling to cool
the room, summer of falling asleep in dampness,
summer of waking

at night when light from the gas station combed
through, pushing green bark spindles through a
missing pane,

summer of drifting off with leaves

on my skin, I thought a greeting from Monterey,
instead of you—

Summer of car-living when the lease was up, summer
of prying the metal spatula into the back door of the
house in order to shower then crawl through the
window to work, summer of fat rain, summer
of cracked window seals,

the summer that, even though I wasn't yet yours, you

drove eighty-nine and a half miles to help me move my
things that had finally been thrown on the curb,
summer of dampness, of blue-eyed waiting

as we sat together one last night,

the summer of night-growing leaves which I might still find
tangled in your beard.

Lunar Cycle/Full Red Moon

I lived in her twice,
Betty was her name, after
my mother who hates what her
middle initial stands for,
my oxidized, clay colored Betty
'92 LeSabre that I inherited
when YaYa got her new Malibu and I got
promoted from the middle of the backseat
to the captain's chair.

In these summers, we are merchants of
abstraction. A trade route plotted from one all-night
diner to the next, exchanging secrets from the four-corner
booths for coffee, tea, and gold
french fries.

Gummed up fuel injectors—
one foot on the brake, one foot on the
accelerator at all times—to cradle her
momentum at red lights, she needs a constant
influx of gas
and so we lie waking,
incubate
behind the dive bar as neon vines
grow through the door seals, weave into upholstery, blanket
of
August-midnight tallow covers us both,
to sweat off in the morning.

I use my sight of night-creepers winding
to recall a modest cargo:

> two pressed uniforms in the trunk, a few
> summer skirts, paint-enhanced jeans and sandals
> from freshman year, sketchbook riding shotgun, and
> the Rebetika mix tape in the deck which always
> reminds me of distance
> from first birth to now under
> sky passing with one broken tail light.

Z.Z. BOONE's fiction has appeared in *New Ohio Review*, *Potomac Review*, *Adroit Journal*, and others. His story, "The Buddy System," was a Notable in *The Best American NonRequired Reading 2014*. His first collection of stories will be published later this year by Whitepoint Press.

Girlfriend

I know her immediately. The dark curly hair, the thin lips, the heavy breasts. Her name is Meg Darnell, and she was what the others at the conference —knowing I was married—jokingly referred to as my "New Jersey girlfriend." Now she's standing in my driveway, white shorts and a lime-green t-shirt, leather sandals and toenails painted silver, holding a bottle of chardonnay.

"Oh, boy," she says when she first sees me.

My stepbrother, Rob, is behind the car and, along with my ten-year-old son, is removing a backpack and a suitcase from the trunk. It's Saturday afternoon, an August scorcher, shortly after two. Jared insists on taking his uncle's bags into the house unaided while Rob walks around to me, smiles, and says, "Hey." We don't hug or even shake hands. We're not that kind of family. "This is Meg," he says.

"We already know one another," Meg says.

Rob looks from her to me.

"We taught a workshop together last January," I say.

"Small world," Rob smiles. "But I wouldn't want to mow the grass."

As soon as we enter the living room, Jared cuts us off, trying to spin a basketball on his index finger. He's plopped the suitcase and the backpack in the middle of the floor in front of the television.

"We gonna shoot some hoops today or what?" Rob asks him.

Jared tucks the ball under his arm and acts as if the thought has just occurred to him.

"If you want," he says.

Becka comes out from the kitchen, drying her hands with a couple of paper towels. Her blondish hair is back in a ponytail and even across the room she smells like fresh basil. She's still wearing her gardening clothes, the worn jeans and the plaid short-sleeve shirt that was mine while it still fit. Becka kisses Rob on the cheek, balls the paper towels in her left hand and holds her right out toward Meg, who introduces herself.

"Why do I know that name?" Becka asks.

"You probably heard it from me," I say, and then I explain the connection.   Becka is the only adult among us who isn't a writer. She's a social worker. Rob is the most successful, his first novel having been made into a film with Tom Hanks. His most recent—which he hasn't even finished yet—is involved in some kind of bidding war among publishers. I teach at WestConn and write short stories that wind up in literary magazines that nobody reads. Meg's in the same boat, teaching at George Mason University in Virginia. Right now, there's a palpable discomfort within the room—to me, anyway—but finally I excuse myself, pick up the suitcase, and start for the guest room down the hall. Rob, with the backpack, follows.

"So how well do you guys know each other?" he asks when we set the bags down just inside the bedroom's doorway.

"Casual acquaintances," I say. "Two weeks in New Jersey last winter."

"As long as that's all it was," Rob grins.

I ignore the comment and ask him how much he likes this woman. He tells me she's okay, nothing really serious. We go to the linen closet outside the guest room and I hand him a couple of towels and a facecloth. He thanks me, takes them into the bathroom, and shuts the door.

Outside, I can hear Jared, impatient and transparent as ever, loudly bouncing his basketball in the driveway. I'm a bit less active with him than I probably should be, so when Rob shows up, he's like a puppy that's been tied to a fence too long.

In the kitchen, I find Becka putting the wine in the refrigerator while Meg stands next to her holding a glass of iced tea.

"We're going the unhealthy route tonight," Becka says. "Big fat cheeseburgers on the grill, corn slathered in butter, 'Death by Chocolate' for dessert."

"Sorry, Dr. Oz," Meg says, and, for some reason, Becka laughs at this.

I watch my wife, bent over and rearranging things on one of the refrigerator shelves, and instantly I feel the way I did when I was a kid and everyone was in on the joke except one poor, naive schmuck.

It is not uncommon for my stepbrother to stop by on any given weekend. He'll call the night before, request permission (which we always grant because Jared adores him,) and by Saturday afternoon he'll be trotting out some new girlfriend, or some female literary agent, or somebody he's met at a reading earlier that week. Rob - a guy who couldn't scare up a date for his own senior prom – is a man that success has made not only rich and desirable, but confident and a bit of a show-off.

We were teenagers in Baltimore when our mother died —me a senior in high school and him three years back. I left for college in Boston and he stayed, living there in the same house where we were raised. Still, to this day. He says he likes to keep an eye on Wayne, who was never that healthy even when he was married to our mom. Wayne is Rob's bio-dad, my stepfather. Needless-to-say, I am not a huge Wayne fan.

But none of this explains why my stepbrother chooses to drive five hours to our house in Danbury just about every other week. Not when he could just as easily pop these women in some motel room off the beltway and save money on the gas.

"Is he bringing his chick of the week?" Jared will ask when we tell him Uncle Rob is coming up for the weekend.

"Doesn't he always?" I say.

"Remind me to burn that bed when I inherit this place," Jared will say.

Our house is small, but affordable. There's an outside deck, the end of which wraps around a four-foot-deep aboveground pool. It's tacky, but it was in place when we bought the house six years ago. Whenever the weather accommodates—which in Connecticut isn't that often—Becka goes out and swims circular laps for what seems like hours.

Rob has told Meg to bring a swimsuit, another incentive he uses at times like this when the temp hits 90. She wears it now, a black one-piece, as she lounges on a plastic chaise and drinks a bottle of beer. I'm familiar with her body. It's full and lush—a pound or two could obviously drop off—but her sexuality is undeniable. I look over at my wife, seated next to me at the small round cocktail table. She wears a red two piece bathing suit, her slender body as tight as an inflated tire, a woman you might see on some television infomercial demonstrating the EZ Glide Tummy Tucker, or some such piece of junk. Becka sips at a glass of Pellegrino with a slice of lime floating above the ice cubes. She's given up alcohol thanks to her doctor's suggestion and an elevated GGT level.

Meg is talking about the time she took her four-year-old daughter into college and tricked some kindhearted freshman into being the child's guardian while she attended a departmental meeting. To me, the story makes her seem manipulative and not particularly maternal, but Becka seems enchanted by it.

I glance over toward the driveway where my stepbrother allows my son to beat him in a game of "Horse." Sweat stains both the front and back of Rob's gray t-shirt, and every shot or two, he walks over toward the deck steps where he's left his bottle of beer.

"So how did you guys hook up?" Becka asks.

Meg and I exchange a look before simultaneously realizing she's talking about Rob.

"He came to George Mason and did a reading," Meg says. "I got stuck with picking him up at the airport, and by the time we got through baggage claim he was already hitting on me."

"That's our Rob," I say.

"Well I'm ducking in," Meg says as she stands and heads toward the pool.

"I like that idea," Becka says. She gets up and grabs her goggles from the deck railing. "You?" she asks.

"You two go ahead," I say, holding up my glass. "I've got a martini calling my name."

I watch as Meg lowers herself from the aluminum ladder into the water. Becka joins her and they both squat so that they're up to their shoulders, arms spread and heads back, eyes aimed at the sun.

In the driveway, a basketball hits the backboard and I turn my head to watch it drop through the hoop. "That's horse!" my son shouts.

"You got me," Rob says. "Jumpin' J-Rod strikes again."

The conference was in Toms River, and went under the title Jersey Shore Writers' Workshop. It was run by a husband/wife team—Celeste and Franco Bittermann—who'd found a string of cheap, seasonal cottages that the summer population was only too happy to rent out. The "Main House," which was the biggest cabin with the most insulation, served as the general meeting place, while the others were used for both student and staff housing.

I'd gotten their flyer in my faculty mailbox just before Thanksgiving. They offered a thousand dollars as an "honorarium to selected writing instructors interested in a mid-winter getaway on the picturesque Jersey shore." The residency fell neatly between fall and spring semesters. I figured we could use the money after Christmas, so I emailed my resume.

I'd been to a couple of these things in the past, so I knew the terrain. A lot of untalented hobbyists, a handful of drunken faculty, a good amount of indiscriminate pairing up. And I'd been careful until that point, if not with the booze, at least with keeping my pants on.

So here's the short version: The first night, at the "Meet and Greet" in the Main House, I'm introduced to Meg and immediately attracted. We talked about our mutual interest in Victorian literature, and about fifteen minutes in, she mentioned the fact that she'd recently been divorced. I took this as an obvious indication that she was fair game. But then I lied to her. Stupidly. I admitted that I was married, but I claimed we were having problems. On the spot, I concocted this story about a relationship in which the couple had grown more and more distant. The husband was trying to hold it all together—for the sake of their son—but the wife had recently admitted a sexual preference for members of her own gender.

That night, Meg and I wound up in my cottage with a bottle of scotch filched from the "Meet and Greet," in a bed so squeaky we had to drag the mattress onto the cold, wood floor. Other than the workshops we had to run, and the bullshitty mingling we had to do, Meg and I were pretty much all-in-all the entire time.

Let me say right here, right up front, that I may have said a thing or two that could have easily been misinterpreted. In the heat of sexual combat, I might have even told the woman I loved her. I'm not beyond that; it wouldn't have been the first time. And Meg was no dewy-eyed ingénue, either. "Love-zlub," she told me one night as we walked on the frigid beach holding gloved hands. "We're just doing what the Victorians called dabbing it up. Just joining giblets."

I insisted she was wrong. That we had something here. I told her I pictured myself playing with her kid. I said that I wanted to pursue our relationship after the conference, and although she kept an emotional distance, by the end of the two weeks, she gave up the struggle and allowed me to reel her in.

"Thanks heaps," she said during our last night together. We were out on the porch of the Main House alone, huddled under a blanket. "The last thing I wanted to do," she told me, "was come here and turn into a quivering seventeen-year-old again."

I thought about her for a few days after I got home, but that was it. I made no attempts to contact her; why would I? I didn't feel great about what I'd done—more like a kid playing Ding Dong Dash—but these things are what they are. Meg emailed me a few times, until finally, I guess she got it. And believe me. I accept responsibility. I was a misleading creep. But I was also trying to be romantic, which I guess you could say was my biggest mistake.

By dinnertime, I've switched over to red wine, and I'm bombed. I've managed to roll the gas grill out to the center of the deck, fire it up, go inside and find the five formed burgers in the fridge. I've taken everyone's order. Meg has told me that she wants hers as close to raw as possible, which I take as some kind of thinly veiled dig.

I watch the beef sizzle, but my attention is actually on the two women. Still in their wet bathing suits, Becka sits on a plastic deck chair while Meg, standing behind her, braids my wife's hair into a single, thick rope.

"I would kill to have this hair," Meg says.

When she's finished, Becka walks over to me, turns her back, displays.

"How do you like my new look?" she asks.

"Cool," I say, when in fact I think it makes her look like some goat herder just down from the Swiss Alps.

"I'm going to change into something dry," my wife says, looking away from me and over at Meg.

"I'll be in in a sec," Meg tells her, and I watch as my wife opens the sliding glass door, smiles and swings her braid as she enters the house, then rolls the door closed.

"So..." Meg says as she gathers the comb and the rubber bands. "Feeling awkward yet?"

"Congratulations," I say. "Mission accomplished."

She takes a few steps closer to me, stops within arm's reach, keeps her voice low. "What is that supposed to mean?" she says.

"I'm just curious," I say. "How did you know Rob was my brother?"

"I didn't."

"Right."

"You guys don't even have the same last name," she says.

"So all this is just a coincidence?"

"I was as surprised as you were."

I shake my head, flip the burgers.

"You're worried I'm going to say something," she says.

"Are you?"

"I don't know," she says. "You did fuck me over pretty well."

The glass door is quickly slid open and I almost expect someone to say, "Ah ha!" But it's only my son, who dashes onto the deck, all smiles.

"I was Sheamus," he declares, "and I made Uncle Rob's Undertaker tap-out!"

Rob follows, puts an arm around Meg, and says, "I fell victim to the computerized cloverleaf."

I'm about to ask if somebody can shut the door and keep the air conditioning inside when Becka reappears, still in her bathing suit, carrying a couple of glasses of chardonnay. She hands one to Meg, and takes a sip from the second.

"I thought you weren't supposed to drink," I remind her.

"Special occasion," she says.

The mosquitoes begin arriving, so we move dinner inside. Becka offers Jared the option of eating in front of the TV, which—since professional wrestling is on—he happily accepts. I'd have preferred him joining the adults around the kitchen table, another buffer, one more distraction.

During the meal, Meg mentions her ex-husband. He was a drummer in some third-rate rock band called "The Pugilists," occasionally getting paid to give music lessons, more happy staying home with their baby and watching cartoons while she worked.

"About once a week, he'd find some excuse to leave the house. Always at night. He needed to go over some new songs with one of the other band members. He had to run up to the mall and get some dampening gels. He wanted to drive around for a while to clear his head. And then one night around ten the phone rang and it was their lead singer Missy. She told Jeff that her car had gotten a flat and asked if he could come and help her out."

"Isn't that what triple-A is for?" Becka asks.

"He said her cell phone was almost dead, and that she was in a bad neighborhood, and she was scared to leave the car."

I notice Becka refilling both white wine glasses while Rob picks up his plate of food and goes in to join my son. I pour myself another merlot and wonder how I can move this conversation in another direction.

"When he got home after midnight, it hit me. I know the smell of a man who's been changing a flat tire, and I know the smell of a man who's been with another woman."

"Boys will be boys," I say, and immediately regret it.

"Listen," Meg says, not even looking my way. "I'm not stupid. Adam meets Eve and these things happen. But when deception is involved, the punishment needs to fit the crime."

"So what did you do?" Becka asks.

Meg smiles.

"Did you ever hear the noise a full set of drums makes when they're pushed down a flight of stairs?" she says.

After Jared goes to bed, somewhere around 9:30, Becka breaks out the Scrabble game. I'd hoped by this time that Rob—fueled by alcohol and red meat and sugar—would have steered Meg into the guest room and that would have been it at least until morning. But the two women are as animated as wasps, sitting at the kitchen table, giggling as they set out the game board and begin flipping the wooden letter tiles face down.

Somebody decides we should play doubles, the home team versus the visitors.

Maybe I'm being paranoid, but once the competition starts I think I detect Meg using her letters to deliver subtle jabs. After I spell out "ART," she makes it "ARTIFICIAL." She turns "HONEST" into "DISHONEST." "SIN" becomes "INSINCERE."

I anticipate her going Victorian. Spelling out something like "CLICKET." And then, challenged by Becka, offering the definition.

It means 'desiring coitus,' she might say. In heat. As in, 'Last January your husband and I were in a constant state of clicket.'

"I think Robbie struck gold this time," Becka tells me as we get ready for bed. I can hear her pulling the covers down, sliding in. She sleeps naked, but refuses to have sex unless the house is empty. These days, that's close to never. I finish flossing in the tiny master bath, rinse my mouth in the sink, walk in and join her.

"I'm not so sure," I say as I put on a fresh pair of boxers and a new white undershirt with the fold creases still in it.

"Why? What's wrong with her?"

"She strikes me as a bit unbalanced," I say as I slip into bed.

"You old cynic."

I lie on my back and stare at the ceiling. "Just my opinion," I say.

"Based on what?"

"Based on the fact that when we worked together, she claimed one of the other instructors was coming on to her. It turned out to be totally untrue."

"You never mentioned this."

"It's the way innocent people's reputations get ruined."

Becka reaches over me toward the lamp on my bedside table. "Well, I like her," she says, and after a flick the room disappears.

The next morning, noise from the kitchen gets me up. I go downstairs and find Rob and Meg already dressed, trying to figure out the coffee maker. I've put on my same clothes from the day before, shorts and a stripped polo shirt, both of which still smell like smoked meat.

"I got a call from my agent around six this morning," Rob says. "I don't think the woman sleeps."

"Everything okay?"

"She wants to meet me for lunch. Apparently the new book just sold."

"Wow," I say, my envy hopefully not showing.

"She wouldn't give me specifics," Rob says, "which is good. I guess she wants to be there to see my reaction."

"Let me do that," I say, taking the aluminum carafe from him and finding the filter basket among the dishes in the drain board.

Becka walks in a minute or two later, blue silk robe, hair still braided. She congratulates Rob when she hears the news, suggests that tonight we find a babysitter and have a celebration dinner somewhere expensive.

"I think we're just going to head back," Meg says. "My daughter is with her dad and I'm supposed to pick her up in the morning."

Becka's face falls like some kid watching her only friend heading off for summer camp.

"So why don't you come with us?" Meg says to her. "While Rob's with his agent, we can haunt Manhattan."

"Great idea," Rob says. "You can grab a train back."

I point out that our son has this birthday party—his buddy Carlo, two blocks over—at 1:30, and Meg asks why I can't take care of it. With three sets of eyes on me, I look over at Becka and shrug like some helpless dolt.

"If you really want to go," I say.

I don't much like being on my own, never have. I can sequester myself in a room for an hour or two, try and force myself to be creative, but in the end, I'm always relieved to see my son getting off the school bus, or my wife pulling into the driveway. Rob is the opposite. He's never had a serious relationship that I'm aware of, and admits that he's spent more time in bed with his laptop than he has with any female. I don't know. Maybe that's why he's so successful.

Alone in the house, I struggle to keep my mind off what I fear is going on: two women—perhaps at a cafe, maybe in some fitting room trying on clothes—begin a conversation. *I like you*, one of the women is saying, *and I think there's something you ought to know...*

I vacuum the rugs, and dust the bookcase in the living room, and put away all the dishes. Things that I hope Becka will notice, that will please her. I wish I hadn't cut the grass two days ago; she loves the smell in the air when I first do that. I try and watch television, but my concentration is shot. It's 3:30, a half-hour before I'm scheduled to walk over and pick up Jared.

Even if the worst happens, I tell myself, I can wiggle out. I'll deny it. Laugh it off. I've already planted the seeds

of doubt, now I just need to water them. I'll turn the guilt around. *Why would you choose to believe somebody you've just met over me? I thought we had more than that.*
Like most married couples, we've presented the hypothesis. We'd only been married a few months—at that point where we couldn't get enough of one another—when I asked Becka what she would do if I cheated.

"I'd have to go away for a while," she had said, "until I was sure I was the only one you wanted." And then it was her turn: "What if it was reversed?"

"I guess I'd eventually forgive you," I said. "But things would never really be the same, would they?"

The phone rings. I imagine it's my wife calling to tell me she knows. *I am so disappointed! How could you do this?!* I picture her standing on Fifth Avenue, cell phone pushed against her ear, crying and red-faced, with her free hand balled into a tight fist. People on the street walking around her as if she's Moses parting the Red Sea. And I see Meg standing next to her, a supporting hand on my wife's shoulder, her head nodding with understanding and compassion.

But it isn't Becka calling. It's Jared. The magician got tied up in traffic and has just arrived, and my son wants to know if he can stay an extra half-hour.

She comes in around five. She's happy, energized. She's bought t-shirts for both Jared and myself: his with a caricature of a pickle ("I'm Rather a Big Dill,") mine with a drawing of a human arm bone ("I Found this Humerus.") Jared slips his on immediately and asks if he can bike over to Carlo's house and show him.

"Just hurry back," Becka says. "Maybe your father can call for pizza."

With Jared gone, I ask Becka how her day was. Turns out it was all about Meg. Meg this, Meg that. Evidently, Meg has kept her mouth shut. Let sleeping dogs lie. I'm relieved and begin to think in clichés: I've lucked out; I'm safe at home; I dodged the bullet. If Meg has the same shelf life as my stepbrother's other girlfriends, she's already past her pull-date.

"What would you think of this?" Becka says. "What would you think if I went down to Virginia over Labor Day weekend and spent a few days with Meg?"

"Why would you want to do that?"

"She invited me," she says. "Plus it would give you and Jared some father/son time."

"I'm sorry," I say. "I just don't know what you see in this woman."

"We click," she tells me. "She's the first real girlfriend I've had since before we got married."

Becka slips off her shoes, picks them up, starts toward the upstairs.

"I should text her," she says. "Let her know I got home safe."

I remember I'm supposed to call the pizzeria, but as I reach for the telephone, I suddenly get it. This is Meg's revenge. She'll draw this out for as long as she can, delighting in the absolute torture she's putting me through. She'll never say a word. She has another plan: elbow me aside while slowly funneling away my wife's devotion.

When I walk upstairs and into the bedroom, I see her standing in front of the dressing mirror, head down, undoing the braid with her fingers. She's humming a song I've never heard before.

"What would you like on the pizza?" I ask.

"Anything but anchovies," she says.

"Becka?"

She looks up at the mirror, smiles at the reflection standing behind her.

"I have a little something to tell you," I say.

AIMEE MACKOVIC earned her BA from Wake Forest University and her MFA in poetry from Spalding University. Her work has appeared in *Elephant Journal*, *Main Street Rag*, *The Cresset*, and others. She was the "noteworthy poet" in *UCity Review's* Issue 9. She lives and writes in Austin, Texas.

Alchemy

Ten o'clock at night on the last day
of November. Austin, TX. We're sitting

on a cafe patio under an oak tree strewn
with cheap lights. We sit outside because

we can, because tomorrow is the first day
of the last month of the year, because timing

is everything. I plunk my tea bag
into the teapot, watch it stain the water. I want

to tell you that I know we've been circling
this moment for lifetimes. The air is thick

with angels who have led us here. It takes
a few moments for the water to surrender itself

fully to the tea leaves. That, my love, is us.
When I ask what brought you here, you say

change, and I answer the same.
The waitress has some arm tattoos that will soon

be covered in winter clothes. But not tonight.
Tonight wafts amok between the past and present

with expert precision, and I'm gobsmacked
by the mix of it all. It was always meant to happen

this way, this ember spark. And when you walk me
to my car, pulling me into a hug that lifts me

from every conceivable type of ground, did you not
feel us being doused in a most perfect alchemy,

a most delicious of cosmic interventions?

Requiem For a Fall Day

It is the season before the season
of death. Everything is decaying in preparation
to return to the earth to wait for sweet
awaking - the leaves blush and fall, scorch
the ground with their defiant crackle. The air chips
down to the marrow.
        It rains
the day you cancel coffee, and the winds tell me
we will never reschedule.

        I've died this death
exquisitely so many times in a rainbow of ways,
the fire-sting warms me.

There exists a blind screech owl
whose huge marble eyes shine like two galaxies
        swimming with stars burning
against a night turned lapis. I can't help wishing

to be this owl, to be blind

to some things. Six months till spring, till warmth -
a concept lost to me. Universe, whisper me

        your will, fill me with borrowed light,
I promise to believe in the power of the promise

of spring buds to come, even through the brittle ice.

ALAN WOR is the pseudonym for the broken down superhero who lives inside Ryan Row. His short fiction appears in *Writings on the Wall*, *The Kokanee*, *Danse Macabre*, and elsewhere. He lives in Berkeley California and is currently studying Creative Writing at San Francisco State University.

I Set the Jazz

I keep her in the corner of my eye. A string quartet stuffed up on a tiny stage mangles a slow boogie, but she lets the party shift around her like the colorful squares of a Rubik's Cube. The men wear oil-spill tuxedos and smoke cigars, and the women wear silver dresses, which cling to the curves of their bodies like wet towels, and they laugh into the backs of their hands. But she drinks a long flute of something pale yellow and doesn't speak to anyone. She wears her dark hair up, and her dress is cut along the leg to reveal the mellow curve of her thigh. Her perfume smells like Irish whiskey and freshly showered skin. Her black eye shadow and bloody sunset lipstick are striking against her paper-pale complexion. I stare at the bend of her ankle, rising from the red straps of her shoe. Her cigarette jumps up and down, like the needle of a lie detector, when she speaks.

And I tell her all kinds of lies.

I tell her she was made for that dress. It fits her like a second skin. And I tell her she knows how to smoke a cigarette, delicate and with the tips of the fingers and lips. I move us out to the balcony. Behind her, the city shines like a dark river running with flecks of glinting fool's gold. I point out constellations in the city lights. The Bottle. The Running Man. Dick. I make her laugh into the back of her hand. Later, after more champagne, she laughs without covering her mouth and I see her small teeth are bent and off-white.

I tell her I know her. I've been where she's been. I've ridden that bus, with the green windows and blue plastic seats, from Greyhound Nowhere to Big City Broken. I've stared at my reflection in the window of a warmer place. My feet have beaten the street, and I've said so many things I don't believe. To the preacher on 23rd and Ash, so he will stop following me with his feral green eyes. To the old woman in 6G, so she will keep bringing me left-over potato chive soup and sour rolls. To my father, through a pay phone heavy on my shoulder, while I watch the rain slide down the outside of the Plexiglas booth. *Yes, I still have grandma's silver cross. I wear it around my neck.* To myself, so I can sleep hard and forget my black dreams.

I tell her she doesn't have to worry anymore. I am that sterling wish. I am that bright city. I am that princess dress and those crystal heels, and I will take her dancing in jazz ballrooms with polished copper floors and hot, wet air alive with jagged knives of music. I tell her I will wrap my silk sheets around her dreams at night. I tell her I will watch her as she sleeps and bring her coffee, as rich and smooth as butter, when she wakes. I'll let her drive my 52' Lincoln Cosmopolitan, power seats and glittering chrome. I'll drive her to the ocean, and we'll lay on the sand like kids, our toes lapped by salt waves.

I tell her she's my sapphire. My treasure. My dark liquor. The dream I have every night.

I know she picks up on them, these recited words like the worn lyrics of a choir hymn. I can see it in her cat's eyes and her sharp bones that only show themselves at her bent elbows and the points of her knuckles.

But she wants everything I'm selling, and I'm offering it so cheap.

That first night, she lets me take her from behind, against a thin wall layered with curling paper covered in a print of dull purple flowers. It's her place. Her one room and her bed that folds into the wall. Her half bottle of gin in the dresser, which we drink after, straight from the bottle. Passing it back and forth like men on the street. They're her cigarettes. But it's my golden lighter.

She hangs her borrowed dress carefully in the shallow closet, then asks me what I want to do now, sticking out her chest just enough so that her bare breasts catch the city light from the window. I can read her mind. I can see all the places in her head, even the ones she hides from herself. *What's one more little lie between friends?*

Not much.

That first night, I show her what city snow feels like. Dirty and cold but high and clear as it falls. That powder. I let her roll in it while I watch, bare-chested, from her bed. When I bump, she bumps. But I bump easy. I cut lines of flour for myself, and she's eager to look as savvy as I've told her she is.

I think I'm starting to feel it.

I can tell when she really starts to feel it. Outside, I hear the cars moan and the night lights sizzle like frying eggs. The breeze is hot and smells like petroleum. Through the walls I hear her neighbors moving. Somewhere, a man yells and breaks a glass.

Her phone rings, and she tells me not to answer it. But it rings and rings and on the twelfth ring she buries her face in my tangle of chest hair and cries. Which is how I know it's her mother. I can see her. Hair up in old pink curlers.

Blue cotton nightgown. Sitting at the kitchen table in the dark, clutching a wooden crucifix and counting the rings.

In the next few weeks, she will want to know me, the way I seem to know her. She concocts theories about my past. I was a corn farmer in Nebraska who, at the age of sixteen, beat a crooked mayor to death with the leg of an oak table after I caught him molesting a little girl. Had to slip names and hit the anonymous city to escape unjust law. I was the son of a banker. But then pops robbed the bank and split with a blond high school boy only a year older than me, leaving his wife and son with a broken piggy bank and a mess of court dates and dirty looks on the street. Maybe I send money home each month. My dad had a problem with the sauce, or my mom slept around or was a paid whore who always told me, *Never do anything for free, Sugar.*

Always, there is something black in my history, and I end up a victim.

I let her invent me.

I don't tell her about my past. I don't show her my apartment and rarely drive her in my car. Sometimes I drop hints like dimes or breadcrumbs. *Heading back to 3rd street, doll. Maybe I'll pick you up a dress.* I give her money for a cab, or the bus, and I pretend not to count it. Sometimes it pays the whole fare, sometimes not. I visit her at Calhoun's, a mostly black jazz club, where she waits tables in fishnet stockings. I order well whiskey and I follow her with my hooded eyes. On her fifteen I lead her into a bathroom stall and push up her skirt. She breathes like nobody ever taught her how. Short, hard. Smoker she is. She pants in my ear and I stare at a bathroom tile that's stained a sticky yellow.

Sapphire. Doll Face. Princess. Heart Breaker.

My names for her bounce off the hard bathroom surfaces like rubber balls. The same way they bounce between the walls inside her head.

She's late, but I make her bump off my stiletto flick knife before she heads back out to finish her shift. For her, I always dress like I'm going to a party. Trim suits and a three dollar polish on my shoes. Black fedora turned just so.

I move her from snow to tar in three flat weeks. She says she thought I was going to take her dancing. *This is dancing, Sapphire.* She trusts me, and I'm not sure why. But I know how to make her dance. She clutches my hand as I trace the veins in her arm with my fingers. I see the clouds in her eyes and the long road to the sea. I sit with her all night and keep her on her side. I feel her small breath with my hand when I can't tell if her chest is still moving. In the morning, her skin is soft and her eyes are crusted shut.

I add rubber tube and packs of disposable needles to her dresser. Burnt steel spoons. Cotton balls. I give her my old lighter, tell her it means a lot to me. It was my uncle's, and he carried it in the war that killed him. Whatever. Her eyes are hungry, open mouths, and she claws my back at night.

She loses weight. Now all her bones show. The waitressing doesn't last. The manager tells her I'm bad news. She should ditch me. Then he hands her an envelope with her last check and a bundle of dirty, small bills. Her tips. Later, I pocket them and tell her not to worry. To never worry again.

She nods without hearing and searches my pockets with her eyes.

I tell her to pack some clothes. She doesn't ask why. I take her for a long drive. I put the top down, and the wind sets her hair whirling out behind us. We leave the city. Fields of orange trees and late sunflowers run by. I don't know what she sees anymore, but I let her breathe the air in motion. The wide sky. Trees and speed limit signs flash by like the blurry moments of our lives. I buy strawberries and peaches off a stand. We eat them by a little river, threaded along the road like a vein of silver. We chase the fruit with hits of bourbon. She starts to tell me about her home town. Her swing on the lemon tree. The powder smell of chalk in the classrooms. Christmas mass at midnight. The clock tower. The way she and her brother would sneak up into it in late summer and play in the moving shadows of the gears and pendulums. The heat that made them strip their clothes, like peeling the skin from ripe tangerines. And since then, she has always been able to tell when someone's eyes are on her.

I tell her to stop. That she's told me this story before. And she's so blazed she can't remember if she has. Peach juice runs down her chin. I can smell the river mud. Fresh earth and a kind of slow rot, like old fruit.

Driving back to the city, the fractured mess of the setting sun behind us, she keeps talking. But the wind whips the words right from the round edge of her mouth. At one point, I think she is screaming at the sky. I pretend not to notice and continue to smoke in the high wind.

In the city, top up, we drive through neighborhoods she doesn't recognize. Corners lit soft and red. Women without faces in ruby shadow. She asks where we're heading. I tell her to take it easy. I tell her the ocean. I tell her Paris. I tell her a party lit by men with bronze skin wearing golden masks and holding torches. I tell her her mother is there, waiting, and she'll rock her to sleep in her arms when we arrive. I set the slow jazz on the radio low, and I tell her she doesn't have to be so hard anymore on the inside. I tell her to close her eyes and when she wakes up, she'll be there.

HEIDI FUHR lives in Minneapolis, where she writes creative nonfiction and graphic narrative. She recently earned an MFA from Minnesota State University, Mankato. Her creative work can be found in *Revolution House* and *Haute Dish*. Currently, she writes articles on fiction craft for the blog *20 Questions Film*.

Daily Grind

I tumble into the dressing room of the strip club bundled up to the chin against the February cold, lungs burning from puffing a smoke in below-zero air on my way to work. The club is tropical by comparison. I tear off my scarf, mittens, coat, and hand-me-down men's snow boots. My socks are mismatched and crusty, my hair is stringy, my armpits are sweaty.

I like to think I don't quite fit in here like the other girls do. I was twenty-five when I started stripping, unlike most of the girls, who were eighteen, sometimes younger. With half a bachelor's degree, I'm relatively educated. I vote. I read books for pleasure. I wasn't sexually abused as a child. I'm a feminist (in theory if not in practice; this job is a temporary fluke). I don't come from a trailer park.

I am, however, here for the easy money, like everyone else. One day, when I've hung up my stripper shoes and moved on to a clothed career, I'll realize that I'm not superior to the natural-born strippers. I'm worse. I'm a heroin addict. I'm so desperate for money, my core values and convictions have gone soft, but my perception of myself hasn't caught up with my reality yet. Most of my coworkers are more genuine than that. They know who they are, what they do, and they *own* it. I'm only a stripper when I'm here, when I'm in (or out of) costume and people call me by my stage name, Entropy. When I'm off the clock, I still call myself a student even though I dropped out of college two years ago. I call myself a writer even though I pawned my computer and lost all my files. I don't even keep a journal. I tell people I work as a cocktail waitress. My actual work duties are an intangible concept, a morbid shame.

One of my colleagues, Sparkle, clops out of the dressing room toilet stall on her six-inch, red plastic platform stiletto heels. She turns her back to the full-length mirror, bends at the waist, and spreads her bronzed ass cheeks apart. "Can you see my tampon string?" she asks. Her body is strangely un-mammalian; every inch of her smooth, plasticky skin is the same Malibu Barbie shade of beige as the little glass bottle of foundation makeup on the counter next to her purse. Her vulva is only slightly more detailed than that of an actual Barbie doll: devoid of hair follicles, all the intricate inner parts neatly hidden by the peach-like cleft of her labia majora, one end of which is punctuated by a clean pink pucker. It's difficult to imagine that her vagina belongs to a living organism at all, that it smells like anything other than a new My Little Pony doll or a box of crayons, that it is, in fact, even an orifice, much less that it requires a tampon.

"Nope. You're good," I say, wiping the thaw-snot from my still-red nose. I imagine that Sparkle should have seams where her legs attach, that I could pop them off to find not bones and ligaments, but injection-molded little knobs that fit into her hollow pelvis. Sparkle and I exist on opposite ends of the spectrum of sex-kittenness. None of our colleagues are quite as airbrushed as she is, neither are they quite as awkward, knobby, scarred, or sweaty as I am.

The throbbing techno bass of Sparkle's song, "Smack My Bitch Up," rises from the stage below. For good measure, she spritzes herself with coconut body spray and scampers down the spiral stairs to the stage.

It's six o'clock on a Tuesday. The dressing room is littered with the trappings of false beauty: curling irons and flat irons and push-up bras and thong panties; make-up cases overflowing with hundreds of garish, glittery lipsticks and eyeshadows; a dozen brands of a dozen shades of industrial-strength concealers; satin bustiers and spandex tube dresses; wigs and extensions farmed from poor Hindu girls on the other side of the world; designer-knockoff purses and faux fur coats slung over the backs of chairs. The smell of Aqua Net, Marlboros, and Bacardi poorly mask the digestive stink of thirty girls who eat nothing but cheap takeout.

I prepare for my first stage set. Five days a week, I sit in this dressing room and wish I could snap my fingers and be done with the hair, makeup, and costumes. It's exhausting. My first week here, the mid-spectrum girls (the only-slightly-airbrushed ones), saw me struggling with my limp hair, bare-bones make-up routine, and banal underwear, and they made me over—not out of camaraderie or goodwill, but out of pity and boredom. I was so pathetic, I posed no threat to them, even after they tarted me up with hair extensions and cat eyes. They didn't realize I'd keep coming back, that the ever-present specter of opiate withdrawal would compel me to learn to hustle like a pro in a matter of weeks.

I strip off my jeans, tee shirt, and crusty socks. I rip a brush through my hair, which is still stringy from the cycle of sweating, freezing, and thawing under layers of wool during my commute through the snow. I swipe on eyeliner and comb mascara through my lashes. I accidentally blink, depositing a line of mascara dots under my eye. I curse and wipe it off, which smudges the eyeliner so I have to start all over again. This is an almost-daily routine. I dig in my locker for the cleanest G-string I can find and scrub it out in the sink, hang it on a chair, and point Sparkle's hair dryer at it. While it dries I put on lipstick the color of Sriracha sauce; it looks perfect until I smoke a cigarette, then it gets everywhere—on my teeth, on my fingers, in my hair. This is why I wear black (well, that, and because it softens the angle of my weird square hips). Over the still-damp G-string, I throw on a pair of black lace cheekies and a tiny black tank top that says "Bob's Java Hut" on the front. I sip from the discreet half-pint of gin in my locker and pull on fishnet sleeves to cover my track marks.

I still look like myself, mostly (well, maybe like myself trying to look like I did at age sixteen, lying under the covers of my boyfriend's single mattress on the floor of his mother's basement while I wait for him to swipe some rubbers from his big sister's purse), until I slip on my eight-inch pink platform stripper shoes. The shoes are the most important part of the costume, the part that transforms a normal woman into a commodity, into walking sex. When I put on the shoes, the rectangular column of my boylike frame is suddenly forced into feminine curves. The body undergoes an instantaneous chain reaction in high heels: the leg muscles are pulled taut, tugging on the connective tissue of the pelvic bone, which tilts the hips down and the ass up, which causes the spine to arch, which forces the shoulders to seek balance by adjusting back and down, which pushes the tits out, causing their fatty tissue to strain against the acetate bra cups and spill over the top in a fabulous display of cleavage. I am instant porn.

Before necessity prompted me to take this job, I couldn't have imagined myself doing it. I've always been awkward, self-conscious, graceless, and oddly masculine. Before this, I was painfully introverted, especially when it came to physical appearance. I could barely wear lipstick or a skirt. I certainly couldn't dance—not even a little. I'd analyze every social interaction, every implicit gesture, because I was convinced I was freakishly defective, both inside and out, and I had to keep up the facade of normalcy. But I took to this job with surprising alacrity. Years later, I'll wonder if I could have picked it up so effortlessly if I hadn't needed the money so badly. I'll tell myself it wasn't just the fear of withdrawal, that it was years of repressed sexual energy being unleashed at once, or that it was the freedom of having permission to turn off my brain and live in my body. Eventually I'll realize that I couldn't have done it if it weren't for the threat of bone-crushing, skin-crawling, puking-and-shitting withdrawal.

We each have our thing: Lacy, two-time regional champion of Pole-lympics, is the undefeated pole-trick master among us. Jasmine is the white girl with a black girl's butt. LaMay is known for her vintage pubic hair; most of the girls tease her, but she's got the "full bush" market cornered. Summer, at forty-two years old, is the seasoned pro. I'm the tall girl. Most tall women, both in and out of strip clubs, prefer low heels, but I wear the tallest. In them, I stand at almost six-and-a-half feet. I command attention in the simplest way, in the way I have since third grade: by sticking up higher, like a mutant corn stalk or a lightning rod. During my first two weeks here, I hobbled around on these shoes like a crippled giraffe, but now I can run, skip, and jump in them. The skinny stiletto heel is an extension of my tibia and fibula; the impossibly small sole is the ball of my own foot, balanced by my own metatarsals. The slope of the insole is so steep, my stripper footprint is a mere five inches long, about half the length of my actual size-ten.

Sparkle's stage set is over. The raspy, classic-rock radio voice of the deejay announces Entropy on stage next. I run down the stairs, sneaking a quick whiff of my armpits on the way (a little ripe, but nothing I can do about it now). Only one customer sits at the counter in front of the brass pole, a guy from India with a neat little stack of ones and a compulsory nine-dollar Coke. I clop across the stage (the plastic platforms of stripper shoes are hollow, so they make a distinctly horselike sound on hard surfaces), taking measured, long steps that make my hips switch theatrically. I don't dance—I never have and I never will; in fact, stripping has nothing to do with dancing. I do a few lazy pole tricks and slip off my top. I step off the stage onto the floor and slide the customer's coke over. This one's classy —he doesn't flinch protectively when I move his stack of ones, like I'm going to snatch his ten bucks without earning it. I climb over the counter, straddle his chair, and press his face into my chest. He smells like caraway seeds and dandruff shampoo.

Some of the girls do well with the young obnoxious guys, the ones who come late on Saturday nights for bachelor parties, who "make it rain" dollar bills so they can pretend they're in a rap video. My bread-and-butter customers are the quiet guys, the ones who come alone and sober straight from the office. They hand out ones to the girls on stage only because it's proper strip club etiquette, a dollar at a time. Unlike the bachelor-party boys, though, they discreetly spend hundreds of dollars on private dances and hope no one finds out.

I climb the pole and hang upside down, held up only by the friction of my skin on the brass. Other than the spotlit disco ball over the stage, which I could touch with my toe from this position, the club is lit only with red and black lights. The lighting is part of the deception; it obscures flaws that makeup, wigs, and spandex can't hide, like the leathery texture of Summer's compulsively tanned skin, the glue that holds Cinnamon's weave on, Diamond's perpetual bruises—courtesy of her "boyfriend" (pimp)—Lacy's still-healing breast implant incisions, and the vein-shaped scars that radiate from the crooks of my elbows.

It's as dead as it always is at dinner hour on a Tuesday. On the couches in the VIP area, one girl naps, another reads a tabloid, and a third eats a gyro. A customer at a table in back pays no attention to anything but his cell phone. Still here after the day shift, Felony collects her fee from her weekly regular. The manager counts the till at the bar and barks orders at the fat waitress.

Like our state governor, Jesse Ventura, the manager spent his glory days as a pro wrestler. It makes sense that he'd end up here; pro wrestling is to violence what stripping is to sex: staged, melodramatic, spandex-clad, and pure fantasy. It's not hard to picture him then, flexing his once-sculpted torso and yelling theatrically into a microphone about how he'll tear his opponent apart. Now, in his forties, he's balding, overweight, and barrel-chested, but, also like our state governor, he still has the pro-wrestler demeanor:

loud and coarse with a hint of blue-collar "Minne-*soh*-dah."
He routinely says things that would get him sued in any
other profession, things like, "Damn, girl. You need to lay
off the Krispy Kremes!" He teases the black girls: "What's
your man's name again, Coco? Jerome? Devondrius?
L'Monjelow? You know you're my favorite nappy-headed
ho." But he has a preternatural charisma that disarms
people when they should be offended. He gets away with it
because he's real; Ironically—though he's made a life out
of fake violence and then fake sex—he's exactly what he
appears to be. The black girls return his remarks with winks
and smiles. His insults and misogynist jabs are met with
giggles and kisses on the cheek, or return insults, which he
absorbs with something akin to grace.

He appears briefly in a chapter of Diablo Cody's
stripping memoir, *Candy Girl,* which one of my coworkers
showed him shortly after it was published. He was visibly
hurt by Cody's description of him as a racist on the verge of
a heart attack. The book, for which Cody claims to have
stripped for a year at various clubs around Minneapolis,
purely for the sake of writing about it, put off a lot of sex
workers. To us, she was an outsider, an amateur, and an
exploiter. She infiltrated our world to mock us for the
entertainment of her readers.

I gracefully fold myself down from the pole and back to
an upright position—a praying-mantis-like move I won't
even understand the mechanics of a decade from now—and
slide off my G-string. The club enforces strict rules
regarding nudity: we have to be on the stage and out of the
customers' reach when we take our bottoms off, but it's
mandatory to take them off—all the way off, not just pulled

down to the knees—during every stage set, without exception. The manager always says, "These people pay to see *pussy*."

I see Chloe leading a customer out of a private booth by his tie. Chloe is sexy, but not pretty. She's thirty-seven and has cartoonishly big tits, the kind that are meant to look fake. She bought them so long ago that the skin around the grotesque, hardened balls looks webbed. Her mouth is ringed by scowl lines that match her tough-bitch stage persona. Everyone says she gives hand jobs in the private booths (that's *her* thing), and that's why she routinely makes five times more money than the rest of us. State law says we're not allowed to make contact with the customers at *all* in the private booths, so hand jobs are illegal. But so is the standard private dance we all give, which basically amounts to dry-humping.

Inexplicably, there are two kinds of customers who like me: engineers and computer programmers. A disproportionate number of them are from India. According to one guy, it's because I resemble a certain Bollywood star. As my stage set ends, I climb down into the customer's lap. "So, are you a computer programmer?" I say.

"Software engineer," he says, confused.

"Let's go have some fun." I take him by the hand and bring him to a private booth. I make him show me his credit card. It's important to make sure the customer has money before giving him a private lap dance. As independent contractors, we're responsible for the club's portion—one third of each lap-dance fee, plus a flat fee per shift—whether or not we collect our money from the customers. Contrary to popular opinion, private dances comprise ninety-nine percent of our earnings; the money we collect on stage is negligible. The manager always says, "Get your money *before* you ride cock." But nothing kills a boner like a trip to the ATM, so I prefer to use my best judgment and collect later. Software engineers are relatively honest anyway, and they always seem to have an accurate idea of their bank account balances.

Like Chloe with her hand jobs, we all have secret techniques in the private booths. Sparkle, for example, is so small she climbs up their chests and straddles their necks so they can breathe in the scent of her Crayola-scented pussy. Mandy puts her head in their laps and blows warm breath through their pants. My secret technique is kissing. I kiss almost every customer who buys a private dance. Full-on on the mouth, with tongue. According to common knowledge, kissing is a rarity in the sex-work industry. Maybe it's because aspiring young sex workers see sullen hookers in movies and on TV saying, "I do *anything* . . . except kiss," and they think that's how it's supposed to be. But I don't care. Because I'm in constant denial about my reality, I won't admit that I do it, even to myself, until years later. It's not that the act of kissing is distasteful to me; I've never been the type who reserves kisses for "that special someone" (that's what blow jobs are for). I like kissing, and I'm good at it. I'm not grossed out by onion breath or bad teeth or chapped lips. But something about kissing customers offends my cognitively-dissonant sense of values, so I never speak of it. Every time I step out of the booth, I forget it happened. Kissing isn't strictly legal, but that doesn't bother me as much as knowing that my partner would be heartbroken, my family would be appalled, and my coworkers would hiss behind my back about my violation of the rules—not the official ones, but the unwritten stripper's code of ethics—just like they do to Chloe, just like *I* do to Chloe. We hiss even though nearly all of us violate some rule in some way. I'll wonder one day if cognitive dissonance is the default mechanism for sex workers.

My deepest shame, though, is that I don't like to think of myself as the kind of person who enjoys kissing strangers for money, that I actually *am* good at this job, not because I need the money, but because I have no sense of sexual propriety. Deep inside, I worry that I *do* fit in here, that I'm no different from Chloe or Sparkle, that the manager's nasty remarks don't really bother me in this context. That Entropy isn't just a wholly manufactured persona, but a genuine part of me.

In the private booth, the software engineer kisses me back, at first inhaling the kisses greedily, then later—when he realizes it's not an error in his favor, that he can have kisses on tap for as long as he can pay for them—he relaxes into it. He accepts the whole range of kiss varieties that I have in stock: whisper soft lip grazing, light tongue contact, wet smooches on his neck, ear lobe nibbles. Our foreheads touch while my lips hover millimeters from his, both of us breathing a little faster like we're enjoying it. I am. He definitely is. Two hundred dollars later, he has to cash out. I give him a hug and tell him to come see me again. I'm pretty sure I cleaned out his wallet until Chloe grabs him and whispers into his ear. He avoids looking at me and follows her back to the booths like a naughty puppy.

After the last customer leaves, I go up to the dressing room with my colleagues. We fling off our shoes, becoming instantly shorter and plainer, reverting back to our human forms (except for Sparkle, whose pedicured feet stay permanently arched, like Barbie's. I imagine that, instead of calling a cab and going home to an apartment after work like the rest of us, Sparkle is tucked back into a giant Mattel box, her wrists and ankles anchored in their places with twist ties, where she looks unblinkingly through the clear plastic panel until her shift starts tomorrow). We wipe off our lipstick. The trash can looks like a hundred poppies growing from a dirty snowbank. We replace G-strings and garter belts with cotton briefs and gym socks. We remove wigs and fake eyelashes and don sweatpants and tee shirts. We burp and fart, and we let our tampon strings hang free, like they were meant to do. We unplug our curling irons, wash our faces, count our money, and smoke. We slam our lockers and race down the spiral stairs to the stage, where the fluorescent overhead lights are on and the fat waitress wipes our sweat off the brass pole with a bar towel and a spray bottle of ammonia. We pull on mittens, gloves, and hats, and we wind scarves around our faces; there is a veritable mountain of crocheted wool between us. We tie the muddy laces on our waterproof, subzero boots while the manager waits to collect his share of our money. After we pay out, we tip him (and the waitress and the bartender and the bouncer) not because we appreciate their services—they make our jobs harder, not easier—but because they'll make our lives hell tomorrow if we don't. We wave goodbye to each other as we get into cabs and head back to our ghettos/trailer parks/cul-de-sacs/gated communities/

condos—"later girl, be safe, take care"—though we don't really care. We don't even know each other's real names.

The ride home is a sort of identity purgatory between Entropy and the various facets of my "real" self. I coyly answer the Somali cab driver's curious questions about my job. I ask him about his homeland before the civil war—he was an engineer in Addis Ababa. He doesn't judge me when I have him go through the pharmacy drive-through window so I can buy syringes. I tip him extravagantly, then save the rest of my earnings for my dope dealer.

YVONNE STRUMECKI is a singer and writer currently living in New York City. She's sung on two national tours (*South Pacific* and *Man of La Mancha*), and received her MFA in poetry from Roosevelt University in Chicago. Her poetry has appeared in Fearless Books' anthology "*Touching: Poems of Love, Longing, and Desire*" and *Another Chicago Magazine* Issue 50, Vol. 2, as well as forthcoming work in *Specter Magazine*.

Moje Młode Lata

Tipping back my martini glass, I grasp at summered raspberries—like ones I once picked in her New Britain backyard. I knew just the right red shade to pop into my mouth. The stains stuck to fingers, cheeks, and corduroys; small fingerprints left behind on tattered brown. The smell of vodka, clear and strong. Poppy seed. Sweet and black. A chokeberry tree whose bundles I crushed underfoot. An old oak arched half over from a freak hurricane that stood its three hour ground. *Nie idź tam.* I wasn't allowed past its bent bark to unknown neighbors' yards beyond; our wind-whipped clothesline, a beacon towards home. A kitchen-yellowed sun. The quiet hum of dough kneaded through pudgy fingers. Hiding beneath the plastic-clothed table, watching flour drop to the floor like dusted snow. *Bądź cicho.* Silent work for the family women. Mama. *Babcia.* Her red kerchief holding back graying blonde as they kneaded. *Pierogi* filled with cheese. Fried onions and oil. Daily lunches packed for father's factory hours; familiar bee-colored words on a hard-hat left hanging. *Kielbasa* and sauerkraut. Friday's fish in red sauce. The smell of tomatoes straight from the vine gives the summer air a Connecticut thickness that floats within me for a second. *Gołąbki.* Rye bread. *Rogaliki* filled with prunes. Sunday night canasta with neighborhood friends. The mixed orange juice and rum I taste now is not built into her layered cake with coffee icing, but a strong bitter better drunk alone.

Ways in Which I Won't

Catching my reflection in
the hallway mirror; a picture of rage
I wish to contain. Shards of broken
glass and sliced knuckles are easier
to clean than a conscience.

The slap sounded on my skin
at a ripe raw age; a child who only knew
of ponies in pretend paddocks, shielding
from storms under a plastic roof, eating stickered-on
hay. Horses scattered on carpeted ground when I heard
the front door open, the heavy breath of hate;
the hand of a man who left a mark, seared
daily into a mind that could not understand

why. Mother quietly carried her
weakness, a powerless position; *love*,
the only excuse for staying. Once.
Twice. Perhaps the third time uttering *I want
a divorce* will be the charm, changing
the way in which she could see the world—
revolving around her for once. No longer begging
for children's milk, every accounted penny holding her
to him, subservient in every wifely way.

Withstanding his leaded hand, so many
scarred years fading. I fight my instinctual fist;
an inherited temper inlayed in each argument

I try to break. Habitual strength, a forced weakness
used to get my way. Pride being the only give in—
for fear of becoming that which I hate most.

AMANDA HUYNH is a born and raised Texan. Currently, she lives in Virginia, where she attends the MFA Creative Writing Program at Old Dominion University. She reads for *Barely South Review*. Her work has appeared or is forthcoming in *The Stone Circle* and *Huizache*.

My Nervous System

is short circuiting. Again
cognitive connections ignite through my brain
as it translates the reflection
of his facial features. He smiled at me. It's all action
potentials. Exciting my neurons,
cell body to synaptic terminals.
Neurotransmitters jump

the synapse like whispers
of middle school girls at lunch

time. Medulla. Get. It. Together. Heart valves
are sprinting a Hot Chocolate 5K. Alveolar sacs deflate
and diaphragm trips with each—*hic*
up-per lobes' expansion and they ache to be unbothered
by another's dysfunction. I'd like to breathe
in
and out. To keep my nerves
under control. Cerebellum, please
right foot. Left foot. Right

in his direction. Oh my
pituitary gland. Do my cones and rods deceive
my optic nerve? He smiled at me.
My vision tunnels and my stomach tornadoes
my breakfast while my face begins to sweat
and my vagus nerve pushes me

to the floor in a table-gasping
vasovagal spell. But when I wake
up his smile isn't there.

Follow Up

Ms. Robinson, 71-year-old female, here for routine care
regarding bladder cancer.
Status post TURBT. No recurrences. Cystoscopy today
showed no local recurrence.

The chair by the window is empty, but I can see an outline
of you: *Car and Driver* magazine in hand, squinting to read
the print before you tell me about the newest Mustang.

I count the tiles on the ceiling to distract my legs from the
stirrups,
but it's quiet. And I hate it. I realize how much music you
made
to fill up a room. You'd say, *The doctor isn't gonna find*
anything.

When the doctor walks in, he shakes my hand, and I hunch
forward
to tell him: you passed away two months ago. The doctor
gives
a hand squeeze before he inserts the scope. The screen
shows

the fleshy pink of my bladder, reminds me of a cave. *It's*
like
the inside of a blowfish, you'd say at every visit. You didn't
know what a blowfish looked like, but you liked the word.

The doctor slaps off his gloves and says, *Everything's clear,
no
sea anemone looking cancer to worry about.* You would
have
laughed, with that deepness found only in a cello's belly.

But I want the doctor to look again. He finished too
quickly.
He must have missed something. I need him to miss
something.

TERRY SANVILLE lives in San Luis Obispo, California with his artist-poet wife (his in-house editor) and one skittery cat (his in-house critic). He writes full time, producing short stories, essays, poems, and novels. Since 2005, his short stories have been accepted by more than 200 literary and commercial journals, magazines, and anthologies, including *The Potomac Review, The Bitter Oleander, Shenandoah,* and *Conclave: A Journal of Character.* He was nominated for a Pushcart Prize for his story, "The Sweeper." Terry is a retired urban planner and an accomplished jazz and blues guitarist – who once played with a symphony orchestra backing up jazz legend George Shearing.

Windswept Plains

The sun shone through the side window and caught her full in the face. Marilyn rubbed her eyes and sat up. The car's stuffy interior stank of baby poop. She checked the back. Ethan dozed in his car seat, his perfect little chin resting on his chest. She covered his bare arms with the blanket, smoothed his hair, pushed the Chevy's door open and pulled herself up, wobbling. Sometime during the night when the moon went down, she had edged the car off the two-lane highway into the darkness. Now, in the dawn's glare she found herself on a gravel turnout, surrounded by an ocean of Nebraska corn.

Closing the door quietly, she moved into the field, squatted, and peed. With only blackbirds and crows watching, she dug the compact out of her purse and stared at her face, red from half-a-continent's-worth of windburn. Somewhere west of Philly, the car's AC had quit. The summer heat had turned her peach-fuzzed cheeks into leather. She pulled a comb through her bobbed blonde hair and turned slowly to study the countryside. Except for a few pump sheds, the rolling plains held no shelter. A smudge of brown smoke hung above the closest rise. She sucked in a deep breath and let it out slowly. A pickup truck pulling a tractor on a flatbed drove past. It slowed for a moment, but kept moving and disappeared over the horizon.

...no cities...no yammering...just sun and the wide open...should've done this months ago...had Ethan in some farmhouse with only the old women watching...

Her son's high-pitched squeal broke her reverie. At the car, she found him wide-eyed and flailing. She opened all the doors to air out the Chevy, changed his diaper and cleaned him with baby wipes before burying the smelly mess under dirt clods at the edge of the field. She unbuttoned her blouse to nurse. His body felt soft against hers, heart beating with a reassuring rhythm. Her muscles relaxed, the tenseness replaced with a warm glow. The silence returned, the tarmac empty of traffic. The heat came on strong. As her baby fed, Marilyn hummed a childhood song and fanned him with a folded newspaper that pictured a long-haired brunette version of her.

With Ethan strapped in his seat, she collected her cigarettes and lighter and stepped outside. She never smoked in any space with Ethan; it might be too late for her but the child deserved a chance. She stared into the fields and thought about the past week: emptying their bank account, buying a used car, listening to TV news in that sleaze-bag motel room, and hardening her heart.

A flock of blackbirds exploded from the greenery. The cornstalks jerked along two rows. Something charged toward her, coming on fast. Marilyn flicked the cigarette to the gravel, hustled inside, and locked the car doors. She fumbled in her purse for the key, inserted it in the ignition and twisted, grinding the starter. But the tired engine wouldn't fire. A girl clutching a fist-sized rock burst from the field and rushed the Chevy. She halted in front of the car and placed a hand on its hood, her chest heaving. She looked maybe sixteen, well developed, with shoulder-length hair the color of corn silk.

"Stop," the girl ordered, "or I'll break your fuckin' windshield." She raised the rock above her head.

Marilyn grasped the steering wheel with both hands and squeezed her eyes shut.

...it always finds me...I never get away clean...like a shadow I can't ever shake...

She raised her head and studied the girl: ragged jeans, a faded pink T-shirt, a pretty dirt-smudged face punctuated with freckles. Marilyn reached inside her purse and grasped the pistol. It felt slippery in her clammy hand, like the last time she'd used it. She unlocked her door and climbed out, held the gun at her side, and moved toward the girl.

The teenager backed away and dropped the rock, stared at the pistol then at her filthy bare feet. She drew a forearm under her runny nose. "Look, I...I didn't mean nothin'... wasn't gonna hurt you."

"What the hell are you doing out here?" Marilyn's voice shook and sounded way too loud.

The girl shrugged.

"What do you want?"

"Water...and maybe a ride."

"Are you from around here? What's your name?"

"Lyn."

"Lyn what?"

"You don't need ta know."

Marilyn paused and stared into the girl's blue-flecked-with-gold eyes. She slipped the pistol back into her purse. "Come on, I've got some water in the cooler."

Lyn flashed a smile before resuming her sullen pout. Marilyn opened the rear door. Ethan let out a howl. She lifted him into her arms then handed the girl a water bottle, watched her chug its contents. She passed her a roll of paper towels. Lyn doused her face liberally and scrubbed at it until her cheeks turned pink, as if they'd been slapped. The water drenched her T-shirt. She didn't wear a bra. The baby stared unblinking at the girl. She reached a hand toward him but Marilyn pulled him away.

"How long have you been out here?"

"Long enough," the girl said.

"You're not gonna tell me much, are you?"

Lyn grinned.

Marilyn opened the passenger-side door and motioned for her to sit. She placed Ethan in his car seat, slid behind the wheel, and gazed westward through the bug-stained windshield. She knew that she was too much of an adult for some freaked-out teenager to open up to. Still, she tried.

"Does your family live around here?"

"Yeah, well...they did."

"Do you have brothers or sisters?"

"Nah, but I always wanted 'em. My parents stopped with me. I guess they quit while they were...behind." The girl's mouth tightened and she looked away. Marilyn paused in her questioning, and then changed the subject.

"What happened to your shoes?"

"Lost 'em."

"I've got some flip-flops in the back you can have."

"Thanks. You got a cigarette?"

"Yes, but you can't smoke in the car...it's bad for the baby."

"Right."

The silence built between them. The girl seemed to study the littered front seat. She grabbed the newspaper wedged next to the center console, unfolded its front page, then stared at Marilyn. Ethan cut loose with a string of baby sounds.

Lyn muttered, "That's about the only age guys are lovable."

"What are you talking about?"

Lyn pointed to the newspaper with its black headlines – *Woman Wanted for Killing Husband, Flees With Baby Boy.* "That's you. You know what I'm talkin' about. That's why you're on this back road to nowhere."

... shit, what do I do now? Damn teenagers can't keep secrets...

Marilyn reached into her purse. It would be easy: order the girl out, march her into the field, put a bullet in the back of her head and let the harvesters chew up her rotting remains. They stared at each other. The girl looked ready to bolt, her goose-bumped arms trembling, arms with dark bruises around the wrists and above the elbows, hands with broken nails and bloodied knuckles.

Marilyn let out a deep breath. "So, am I going to find *your* story on a front page somewhere?"

"Yeah, maybe…but not for a while. We're in the middle of frickin' nowhere, ya know."

"Yes, I'm counting on that. So, are you gonna tell me?"

"No…well, maybe later. We need to get movin'."

"Why would I take you with me? Why would you want to travel with a…"

"You'll need help drivin'…and I look like I could be your daughter, or maybe a younger sister. The cops will be lookin' for you with your kid – not a threesome. The same's true for me."

Marilyn smiled. "You have it all figured out, don't you?"

"I didn't…until now. We need to make it to the coast, to some big city, and get lost."

"Really? Then what?"

"Hey, just get me there and I'll find somebody to hook up with."

"I'm sure you will," Marilyn said and turned the key. The car started without hesitation. She checked on Ethan then pulled onto the shimmering blacktop. They drove into the empty morning with sunburnt arms resting on windowsills, the plains a blur of green and gold. A strong headwind buffeted the sedan and Marilyn concentrated on driving while Lyn slept.

…this actually might work…at least get us to the coast…there's something about her I don't like…but hey, killers can't be choosers…

Near noon, Marilyn pulled the car next to a single gas pump outside some kind of country store with neon beer signs flickering in its windows. Lyn continued to snore. Ethan slept. She climbed out and stretched, staring all the while at her two passengers. Neither moved. A hand-lettered sign attached to a pole read, "Pay befor U Pump."

She pushed into the store, the AC chilling her bare arms and legs, waking her, setting her on edge. A fat man sat in a cushioned chair behind the counter, watching a TV soap. He stared at her. His gaze fixed on her breasts for a few long moments before he resumed his television ogling.

"Give me yer money first before ya pump gas," he said without looking at her. "No offence, lady, but I get too many fools tryin' ta rip me off."

"I understand. I also need to get something to eat. Do you have a restroom?"

"Yeah, outside and around back. Sorry 'bout the mess."

Marilyn nodded and wandered into the store's dark interior. A bar stretched along its back wall. But by the look of the dust-covered counter and empty bottle shelves, it hadn't seen patrons for a long time. Rows of supplies on folding tables occupied the space. A bank of rumbling wall coolers full of beer and soft drinks filled a sidewall. She grabbed two bags of chips, a six-pack of soda, two packaged fruit pies, and a few candy bars and laid them on the counter along with three crisp twenties.

"I'll be back in for the change," she said, "and I'll need some ice for my cooler."

"It's around the side," he gestured. "Look, ma wife is making lunch in back. She can fix ya some sandwiches if ya want. Cost three dollars apiece."

"No, but thanks for the offer."

Marilyn moved to the entrance then froze. The Chevy's front and rear doors on the passenger side stood open. The girl and Ethan were gone. She rushed outside, gazed up and down the highway and at the nearby crossroad with its rusting stop signs. The road stood empty of cars and people. She hurried around the corner of the building and almost collided with Lyn. The girl cradled Ethan in her arms, the baby pressed against her breasts.

"What the hell are you doing?" Marilyn yelled.

"Hey, shut up, will ya. I just got the little guy quieted down. I think the heat was gettin' to 'im so I brought 'im into the shade."

Marilyn's heart slammed against her chest. She forced herself to slow her breathing and waited for the fear to subside. "Sorry. Thanks...thanks for watching after him."

The girl grinned and rocked Ethan gently. "He wants ta nurse. No luck here."

"Yes, if you would pump the gas and get some ice, I'll feed him. I've already given the guy inside three twenties for fuel and food."

"No problem."

Lyn sauntered over to the ice machine, yanked a ten-pound sack from its smoking interior, and disappeared around the corner. Marilyn retreated deeper into the shade and nursed her hungry baby. The calm returned. She felt relieved, and grateful for Lyn's help.

...at least she doesn't treat him like a doll...maybe I can trust her...but not yet...let's see how she does with the change...

Marilyn imagined the proprietor's reaction when the braless teenager pushed through his dirt-smudged door. For a fleeting moment she felt concern and patted her purse, reassured by the feel of the gun. In a short while, Lyn returned.

"Everything go okay?" Marilyn asked.

"Oh yeah. That frickin' letch behind the counter was gonna make a move. But lucky for him, his wife came out from the back. Here's your change. The car's gassed and I checked the water and oil. She's down half a quart, but you can wait 'til the next fill-up."

"Thanks. You did good, and sorry I didn't tell you about that creep."

Lyn gazed at Marilyn nursing. "Does...does that make ya feel good?"

Marilyn smiled. "Yes, it's almost like I'm high. Calms me right down, just like Ethan."

"Have you ever given the kid, ya know, formula from a bottle?"

"Sometimes. But it's not as good for him."

"Yeah, that's what my health class teacher told us. Sorry I can't help ya."

"Don't worry. With your looks, you'll be pregnant soon enough."

Lyn brayed loudly. "My mama always said the same damn thing."

Ethan had finished nursing and dozed in her arms. After burping him, she slid him into the car seat and slipped behind the wheel. Lyn had washed the windshield and thrown away the crap littering the front seat. The girl opened cans of soda and a bag of chips.

"You want me to take her for awhile?" Lyn asked. "Ya know, I've been drivin' since I was fourteen."

"Not yet. Maybe after our next stop."

With the car's sun visors lowered, she drove into the shimmering heat and wind. Golden grain fields had replaced the corn and the land flattened even more below a cobalt-blue sky with mashed potato clouds pushing up on the western horizon. Sometime in the late afternoon, she pulled the car off the highway near a deep gully and an under-road culvert. She unfastened her seatbelt and opened the door.

Lyn stirred. "Why…why'd ya stop?"

"I have to pee. Watch Ethan till I get back, then you can go."

"There's nobody out here. Relax." Lyn leaned her head back and closed her eyes.

Punch drunk from hours of driving, Marilyn grabbed the car keys and her purse and climbed out. She took a dozen steps and turned to stare at the girl and Ethan, motionless in their seats. She walked to the ravine and slid down its bank. Out of sight of the highway, she pushed her panties down and squatted. The wind blowing through the culvert howled like a banshee. A shadow fell across the gully. She jerked to her feet and turned just in time to see Lyn charge down the bank and snag her purse.

"What the hell…" Marilyn croaked.

Lyn reached into the purse and withdrew the pistol and Marilyn's wallet. She thumbed the half-inch-thick sheaf of bills.

"So now you're gonna rob me?" Marilyn asked, her face burning.

"Not exactly." Lyn grasped the pistol at arm's length and pointed it at Marilyn. "My plans have changed. A teenage mom with a kid is an even better cover…and your money will help me disappear."

"But the cops could think you're me."

"Give me a fucking break," Lyn snapped. "We don't look *that* much alike."

"I was only trying to help you."

"Yeah, then why the gun?" Lyn laughed. "Turns out, you had a good reason for carryin' it. Ironic, huh?" She sighted down the barrel.

"Please...please don't. Please...my child..." Marilyn backed toward the culvert, stumbling over the uneven ground.

"Quit whinin'. You sound just like my Pop...my mama had more guts."

A solitary semi roared past on the highway above them. Not even the crows heard the pistol's crack. And the coyotes that crept from the fields near sundown seemed to enjoy their unexpected feast.

DAVE SHORR has a degree in Marketing from the University of Iowa and works as a commercial real estate broker. He started painting and writing poetry after his mom died 3 years ago. He mostly writes whimsical, fun, philosophical and science-related poems. He is the lead singer in the rock band Smashing Pumkin's. He was diagnosed as bipolar after college and found writing a great outlet to express himself. He is divorced with no kids.

An Unusually Good Day

I take my morning walk barefoot, get thinner and the world
begins humming happily

I go into my bank, turn into Jesse James, walk out with a
million and turn back to myself

All the animals in the world, who made love the night
before, especially the fat hippos, walk around with red
lights flashing above their heads

Just before dinner I climb back through time and erase all
evil

Then I go see my shrink who travels with a carnival and tell
her the world is finally making sense and she hands me a
stuffed animal prize from the top shelf

When I finally lay down I see the night sky turn a ruby red
color and I fall asleep naked and shameless with you under
the humming trees of Eden marking the passing of an
unusually good day

SALLY OLIVER has a first-class degree and MA in English Literature from Lancaster University. She has been published in *The Flexible Persona, Blueshift Journal,* and *Riding Light Review,* and is shortly to be published in the second *Fugue* anthology by The Siren Press. She works as a Sales and Marketing Assistant for WW Norton in London and loves to read anything written by Ian McEwan and D.H. Lawrence.

Duncan's Manhood

It was noontide and the evil sun had risen to its highest point. Lady Macbeth was already feeling morbid. Not *depressed* – an observation she earnestly forbade anybody to make. She paced the antechamber, full of ire for the impending riot in Scotland. Words such as *smite*, *plunder* and *crucify* filled her subconscious as she spoke at length with her noblemen. Ross and Lennox avoided her eyes and were anxious to be elsewhere. Only Death met her gaze with his eyeless grin. The sockets were rounded holes of chaos, more perceptive and far-reaching than the eyes of God himself. No. To be depressed was to be a half-wit; a putrid leech on the state when now was a time for action as opposed to weary resignation. Her husband shamed her deeply with his doleful eyes and his wrinkled penis beneath the sheets. He had been ill for some time; many whispered that he was depressed. He was growing fatter. She cringed for his sake.

She was relieved it was noon, for she was glad of a rest. She found the middle of the day a place to withdraw herself from the stately procession of royal life. It was a blank passage which ostensibly joined the rest of the parts as well as dividing them: dining, appearances at court, addressing the townsfolk, dealing with complaints and finances, entertainments, negotiations, wine, trouble abroad, music, rumors, banquets, whispers of war. This part of the day was reserved for her, and she would wander to the highest tower of the castle and fold herself into a dark room, unseen.

Her Lord was *indisposed* to visitors. It was a line she had used far too many times for comfort, and the dignity she craved took a new stumble every time it was uttered. Well, she no longer wished to be his smiling surrogate. She closed the door of the highest room in the fortress and locked it, imagining herself to be alone, though she heard from the distant bowels of the building the discontented mutters of the staff. This room had no windows and so was pitch-black without light. Tapestries padded the stone like soundproof walls within a sanatorium. Men with weft-woven instruments of torture charged across the folds, dying abruptly when the picture ran into a blank space. She disrobed, slipping off her gown of midnight blue; it fell into a puddle at her feet. Her undergarments came next. Then she was as stark as if she had just been born. Her pearly body, still sleek from her youth without having acquired the rotundity of the mother's flesh, was enclosed in the four walls like a fetus within an airless coffin.

Her days were ordinarily filled with death; thoughts, fears, dreams, discussions, debates, memories, idle rumors, bawdy jokes. She tasted death in her mouth and there was nowhere to spit it out, certainly not in public. But perhaps she could here. Here was close, dark like the earth beneath the storm of hooves and men in battle. She ran her hands over her pubis, her hips, her breasts, and luxuriated in herself. The two domes of flesh wobbled less now, much less than before, and the nipples were hard like thorns in twin coronets. She imagined the milk beneath withdrawing to a dark cavern at the end of her blood stream; a pit of dearth and delinquency from which there would be no more blooming, no more beauty. Had she grown less beautiful? No. She watched herself in the mirror many times in the morning, the evening. Sometimes she woke and found herself stumbling across their bedroom to look once again. The face had always been sharp as opposed to soft; high cheekbones stretched the face out so that there was no possibility of the flesh sagging or falling into tender folds. Now the jaw was much sharper, the eyes protruding like naked bulbs with the soil pared back. When she saw her face she saw the clean austerity of power, free of the spoils of womanhood: idleness, ennui, childbearing, hysteria.

Macbeth was failing. He was failing Scotland. He was failing her. It had been a good few years since he had last entered her; at least five or six years since he had achieved orgasm. Or had she imagined it? She moved silently across the room and sat by a great chest which was heavily locked. She searched in her memory for the consummation of their marriage. He had struggled to find her. She had lain on the bed with her legs wide apart, not a little contemptuous of him. He would not meet her eyes because it would instantly confirm his ineptitude, and he was often nervous of looking at her directly. Such a man, to never look upon his own wife! Duncan had rattled off remarkable tales of his feats on the battlefield and yet now, suspended like the arm of God above the opening of a woman, Macbeth could not bring himself to the source. She had wanted lightning, pain. She waited for him to hurt her as she had been warned she would be hurt long ago, and she arched her back, desirous of the sting. He lowered himself without force into her belly, wanting the softness of flesh to assuage his fears of having to penetrate it. That was when she snapped. She reached down for the floundering penis and jammed it hard into herself.

There was no earth-shattering ripple of contact like she had imagined. But she had torn herself open for the first time and she was glad, closing her eyes to the man whose penis she held with biting avarice. It moved between them now like a sceptre of gold. A conductor's baton moving to the beat of the bloodline, no longer part of the man she took it from. It was strange how easily she could isolate this organ of power from the glorified instrument, man, to which it was attached. The climax came, the blood quivered, and she saw a brilliant white light in the heart of her delivery, a symbol of hope which lay not in the penis but in the woman's ability to direct it well.

Lady Macbeth knew they needed a child to keep the throne from sliding between their fingers. For now it was like dressing up a corpse in royal attire; only bones lay beneath the ermine silk as opposed to the bloom of prosperity. And yet she was also secretly glad of having been spared the trauma. It appeared that she was barren. Her womb was a vacuum, a black hole. And though Macbeth had failed to plant his seed in her, she had encouraged him to look further afield, for a bastard was better than nothing. She had dangled a number of pretty maids before him and, with typical foresight and sharpness of perception, had guessed at what took his fancy by placing them in contradistinction to herself. Plump girls, soft and simpering girls, short and stout little virgins with their hands very small so that his cock would fill them better. Girls with breasts that heaved and dropped, sighed and swayed. Even she felt the stirring of lust on his behalf; she was almost tempted to burst upon them in the act and catch him in his element at last, the muscles in his buttocks working furiously. Alas, there was no such opportunity. He never looked twice at any women, though she directed them to solicit his attention at any cost. She despaired. A true king would have lain with as many whores as God had created for him, falling right back into Eden again with every orgasm. Yet Macbeth was still ambling along the wayside like Cain in the desert, waiting on Death.

The chest that Lady Macbeth sat beside was one which she alone had the key to. She took it now from the chain which she hung around her neck and inserted it into the lock. Once she was inside she lifted out a second box; a casket with transparent walls of glass so that the contents were instantly visible to the eye. She dared not tilt the box so that the object would move as she was still afraid of it, though it was entirely dead and had shrunk to at least half its original size. She could only imagine the strength of its odour if she were to open the lid now.

She had surprised herself when she took it originally. Primarily she was pleased with herself for having had the sheer nerve to take it that night. But then, in the event of a death, one tends to act with greater spontaneity than before, as though the mind is so terrorized by the sudden hole created in the fabric of things that it goes a little mad. Mad to confirm its own right to exist.

Once Macbeth had struck the dagger first, she knew she must pay the old King a visit in his bedchamber. She could not place her faith in the killer and felt she had to relinquish her faith in the dead man first. Duncan was always worthy of reverence, even her own, though he was too straight, too Christian for her liking. His method of rule was entirely like a golden age of monarchy in which rulers were pure, self-abnegating, yet entirely male. For his manhood was the stuff of dreams; it had demonstrated itself aptly through war and worship, calamity and courtship. And it hung beneath the codpiece at court, resigned to a period of rest for now before its nightly excursion into the soft red walls of his wife. Lady Macbeth knew that it was necessary to ensure he was completely dead when she stole into his bedchamber that night. Her husband had not reassured her that the deed was sufficiently done, for he was so white when she had expected a glow of carnal recovery from his efforts. Perhaps he had blundered in the butchery and now Duncan was half-alive, half-nothing, crying in the sickly space between the two. *Fool!* The thought reviled her. She took the knife and entered the room herself.

Her first thought was that Macbeth was more energetic than she had given him credit for. There was a great deal of blood; the body was swamped in it, draining it away while drowning in its return. And then she saw the man after seeing the body, the person beyond the anatomical ruin. Duncan was finally a mortal, a weary thing to her. His nightshirt itself, white and wispy like a woman's handkerchief, was a horribly abject thing for a man to place on his back, let alone die in. Oh the disgrace! The red stain on the sheer white was like a woman's first bleed, weeping through the dress.

There would soon be a stir from within the castle, and she had this one last moment to spend with the body alone. She moved closer to the bed and, dagger in hand, pulled the nightshirt away from Duncan's legs, hoisting it up along his abdomen. His head was reclining in a strangely tilted position as if he was watching her, but the mouth was shut tight like a fist, the chin receding into the neck. She got back to work. *Quickly, quickly!* She was afraid of her own hesitancy, it was the death of great men and *Hell waits for no one while God looks the other way.* Strike and let sympathy die with it! She cut into the flesh.

Death had already softened it, yet it still took an age for her to sever the organ from the root, for her hands were lame. She thought nothing while she cut through. Thoughts would only frighten haste away and leave rotten futility in its place. Her brain was therefore empty, a fulsome void into which nothing poured itself, continued to pour itself, until the end of time. Voices were already sounding the alarm beyond the corridor and she heard the servants rousing, yet she thought nothing of it. She heard everything, yet she responded to nothing, felt nothing, saw nothing, had nothing.

By the time she had the bloody lump of flesh in her hands, she was disoriented. How long had she been here in this room? The body on the bed was such a permanent fixture of her consciousness she thought it had been years. She wrapped her prize in a large cloth bandage and departed before anybody saw her. It would have been ghoulish to take a last look at a man who was no longer himself. She was curiously respectful until the last. In times of war we forgive our enemies, for we know that a greater force of enmity beyond the individual, harking back to the head of the bloodline itself, is responsible for the resultant spewing forth of blood. Blood begets blood. Some of it is blacker than the rest. Clots form in the stream and pressure accumulates. The family tree is a series of arteries, violently intercepting one another from the root. The cells squabble for release and at last, the stream flows in a different direction. Lady Macbeth had cut off the source, and blood would change hands once more.

Noontide and the evil sun was still hanging on a pitted sky; its warmth managed to reach the windowless room. The glass box, which lay in her ladyship's hands, was warm to the touch as though to compensate for the lack therein of its occupant. She tilted it slightly and watched it roll to one side. It was as though someone had chopped off God's forefinger and now it lay to rest, curling slightly in a ball, when it had once pointed the way for saints and sinners alike. Noble even in rest! This is where Malcolm and Donalbain, royal descendents, had silently crossed from darkness into light, the bridge across which they had sudden access to all things. Sudden startling access. The tip of which had given pleasure to the woman which received it. A hopeful tip; once surely straight when Macbeth's was so low.

After a while she grew cold and realized that something was watching her. At first she thought it was a prelude to a strange dream, being caught between two states of consciousness. She turned her head and saw a dead man standing by the door. Panic sent ripples across her blood.

This was a giant of a corpse, blocking the doorway. Scarcity of flesh could never disguise such stature, even beyond the grave. Soil still clung softly to the skull, and there were little roots where plants had begun to grow from the vertebrae. The mouth was charred and there were pieces of burnt flesh hanging from the jaw. The sockets watched Lady Macbeth.

She wondered whether to speak. The dead man spoke first.

"My Lady."

She dropped the box to the floor. Glass shattered and Duncan's penis rolled feebly onto the stone before bursting into dust.

"My lady."

"No, don't speak!"

"Dear lady. I forgive you."

Like a trapped animal, Lady Macbeth eyed the door. But she couldn't bear to step over Duncan's manhood. It lay between them.

"I forgive you, my lady."

"Why should you?" she said. She lowered herself into a squatting posture.

"I forgive you."

"Stop!" She reached for her dress and pulled it across the floor to herself. "I'll return it to you! I'll bury it with you. I will do it now!"

The spectre said nothing. The empty sockets brooded over her in thought. She was not sure whether he had come from Hell, but she was certain she was going to be escorted there. Anything, anywhere, but as long as she did not have to meet its eyes along the way!

*

Macbeth heard a woman screaming at noontide. He was skulking in the royal chamber at the time, eager for distraction, anything so long as it was outside of himself. The scream was long and varied in pitch, but never fell short of energy. He ran to the door and followed the sound as it moved along the castle. Eventually it died and he was left with an eternal silence again. Death crawled back into the blank space of his skull.

A commotion was taking place, however, and his involvement was close at hand. There was a riot within the royal household and the servants were all frightened like children. He was eventually approached by Ross and Lennox.

"My Lord, the Lady Macbeth has gone mad."

Macbeth was outraged by the presumption. Such a statement was bold and uncompromising, like a declaration of war.

"How dare you say this? On what grounds?"

They were hesitant to follow it up. Ross spoke first. "She has been seen running from the top of the tower and out into the grounds, my Lord. She was screaming and saying strange things that no one could make proper sense of."

"Who did this to her?" said Macbeth. He turned from one blank expression to the other.

"My Lord," said Lennox, "She was saying she had seen Duncan and he had told her to visit his grave to 'return what she had taken from him.'"

Macbeth felt a wave of nausea enter his brain. The ripples made contact with a recent memory.

"She was also in a state of undress," said Lennox. He was struggling to find the right words.

"She wore nothing, my Lord," said Ross. "And she was carrying her dress as though she had something wrapped inside."

"Have you sent someone to bring her back?"

"Yes, my Lord."

"I shall look for her myself. You say she headed for–"

"Duncan's grave, yes."

Once they had left, Macbeth wandered to the window and looked to see if he could catch a glimpse of a bare figure on the hillside. He saw nothing, but he felt her moving in his mind, making a final departure into the sunset. The horizon was growing scarlet, and Macbeth imagined his naked wife in a hell of her own, for it was no longer something they were both swaddled in together. For he felt himself expanding, growing warm, powerful now he was finally free of her. The new blood came back and flushed out the old. Scotland was in uproar, yet Macbeth had grown bold.

MARIE HEGLER is a graduate of Clemson University and currently lives in Greenville, South Carolina, where she spends her days informing the public on relevant, research-based information about food safety and her nights fretting over the Oxford comma. This is her first published work of fiction. Upon its acceptance, she high-fived herself and did the moonwalk, which she learned as a kid from religiously watching Showtime at the Apollo.

Love The One You're With

She bursts into the office with enough disruptive force and gall to cause a bevy of buzzards to flee a bloody carcass, and then immediately begins a futile rant with "How are you?" But before you can answer, she rolls right into answering her own question. "Well, I'm just terrible. Went to the Chinese buffet last night, and on the way back, started feelin' sick to my stomach. Told Harold to step on it. He let me out before pulling into the carport, and I hauled ass to the door. Of course I couldn't find my goddamn keys. So there I stood, squirtin' like a goose."

This is your aunt—your most embarrassing but also most entertaining relative, which you suppose goes hand in hand. She's short and stocky, built like a junior high linesman and similar to the vast majority of family members, both men and women, on your mother's side. At over six feet tall, you have presumably taken after your father.

Your father was a simple man. He liked baseball, Sinatra, and chewing tobacco. He was a World War II vet and worked most of his life in the administrative office of the textile mill. He had dark, square features and a prominent nose, all of which you acquired. But mostly, he was known for being quiet. He never raised his voice, he never angered, and he never said he loved you. You knew he did, though. After you finished dental school, he squeezed you on the shoulder and said, "You've done good, boy."

You returned to your hometown to open a dental practice, and every six months, your loud, disgruntled aunt from Kingstree makes the trip over for her checkup. At the ripe old age of 90, she has her son bring her to these appointments, and although she's always been slightly off-kilter, these days you can't tell if she is legitimately crazy or suffering from some debilitating, age-related illness. Her stories, both past and present, seem to mix together as if time stands still and is never lost. Not a bad way to live, you consider.

While she speaks of "shits and pukes," you try to ever so nicely usher her towards the back room, away from the wide eyes and gaping mouths of the few patients left in the waiting room.

"Aunt Millie," you say, "Why, you look fit to be tied. Why don't you just relax right here while I take a look at your teeth." She does.

She asks, "Where's Pa?"

You say, "Pa's dead. You remember, don't you? Roger and Larry found him in the garden, face-down."

"Oh, right. Where's Harold?"

"Harold's dead too."

She pauses before saying, "Good. I'm glad he's dead."

Harold was her husband, who she was married to for what she denotes as "an eternity" before he died of a heart attack, propped up in a rocking chair with a cheap bottle of whiskey in hand and an eerie smile on his face. You know he too is probably glad to be dead.

You realize kids these days have a different perception of marriage. They think it's all comfy and cozy—hard work, yes, they'll sometimes gloat. But what the heck do these spoon-fed know-it-alls know about hard work? None of them have had to work 12-hour shifts in the mill amid the deafening noise, choking dust, and overwhelming humidity, or in tobacco fields crawling on their hands and knees down the rows and pulling off the suckers. The most these lazy bastards have done is bagged groceries for nice old ladies in air-conditioning or sat behind a counter watching movies at a video rental store.

And love, you know, is not a fuzzy feeling or even a wistful longing. It's not a feeling at all. It's putting up and dealing with, smiling and crying through it all, and all with someone else—someone who isn't you and doesn't think like you. These little Facebook fuckers are in for a world of surprise. Just wait, you want to say to them, just wait 20, 10, or hell, maybe even 5 years, and then tell me you don't roll over and see the same person and think almost immediately, "You again?"

You and your wife are another story. You won't go into the dirty details, but you had to tell your daughter—when she turned the respectable age of 13—that her mother wasn't your first wife. You didn't tell her that you actually met while you were in dental school. She worked in the school's library, and you were married to your high school sweetheart at the time. Things happened.

Later, at your father's funeral, you saw her—the first wife. She had always been close to your father. And for a brief moment, you wondered if you made the right choice. You asked your friend, the doctor whose practice shares a parking lot with yours, this very question. He squinted his eyes even more than they naturally squint and said, "Hell man, that's like asking me whether I want a whiskey or a bourbon. They're practically the same dame. You definitely have a type, and it's not just living and breathing."

He was right. You have always liked short women. Both your wife and your ex were around 5'2" with an ample chest, sturdy rear, and curly auburn hair. You like to tower over them, and sure, you could make assumptions as to what that might mean or what kind of person that makes you. But you also wonder if it had something to do with your mother, who held distinct similarities to the fiery, pint-sized women you've loved and left over the years. Yes, the mother that abandoned you at 10 years old to run off with a sleazy insurance salesman, who always smelled strongly of Brut cologne and had a habit of constantly fiddling with the gold signet ring on his pinky.

When you were 12, your mother tried to talk you into moving to Arizona with her and Randall-you-can-call-me-Dale-or-Dad. You called him nothing and told your mother you didn't want to live in the damn desert. When she asked you where you picked up the foul language, you told her it wasn't any of her damn business since she was the one who hadn't been around. She kissed you on the forehead and told you that you would always be her baby boy. You wanted to cry. You wanted to hug her tight and never let her go. But you only said, "We'll see," and then left the room.

She's still alive, though she rarely comes back around these parts. You talk to her on the phone twice a year on Christmas and Mother's Day, but you haven't seen her in over five. Randall-you-can-call-me-Dale-or-Dad has been long out of the picture, but she stuck around the West Coast.

Her skin has turned to wrinkled leather, something you'd never thought possible from the smooth, fair complexions of her kinfolk. She's the black sheep of the family, which is a pretty big feat considering that side of the family, between the booze and impromptu hell-raising, is made up entirely of black sheep. But she's the blackest of the black because she up and left for good.

You rush through Aunt Millie's gaping mouth. A vigorous cleaning and two composite fillings later, you are ripping your truck through the twists and turns of the back roads to get home. Dust settles overtop the light layer of pollen on your truck, and your head is pounding. Conway Twitty's "You've Never Been This Far Before," a song you've insisted be played at your funeral, blares on the radio. It's 3:15 on Friday afternoon, but more importantly, it's April, the month dedicated to the stalking and killing of turkeys.

You work all the time, and when you're not working, you hunt. Quail, deer, turkeys, squirrels—it doesn't matter. You're a man that accumulates hobbies, never dropping one for another but rather adding on to the ever-growing list. You have two boats—one for fishing and the other for cruising and boozing, two trucks—one for driving to work and the other for driving long distances, two motorcycles—both for no good reason, a four-wheeler, a golf cart, and your newest baby, a 1966 Pontiac GTO Convertible, not to mention, the plethora of guns, golf clubs, fishing rods, and yippy squirrel dogs. Since your father spent his whole life working towards a retirement he never got to enjoy, on account of the heart attack, you are determined to live now, spend now, and have fun now.

You know why your wife never complains of all your activities and hobbies. You know why she just nods when you say you're gonna buy this or do that. She knows your type, and she's aware of her resemblance to your first wife. She's not stupid. She'd rather you be consumed by hobbies than by another woman.

She is also your boss. When your daughter was old enough to fend for herself, she came back to work with a vengeance, or maybe just to keep an eye on you. It was as if she knew exactly when you were getting antsy and wouldn't let you out of her sight. The hygienists she hires are never under 5'3". Mostly, they are either sweet older ladies or skinny blondes, which have never been your type.

She has good reason to do so since you did cheat on her years ago when your daughter was just a toddler. It was only a two-time thing or three if you rounded up. You met the girl at a dental clinic on John's Island. She had skinny legs and freckles that covered the top of her nose. She wasn't anything special. She was just there and easy, and you were young and stupid.

Your wife found out in a jiffy. It was as if she sniffed her on you the moment you walked in the door. The next day she sat you down, and without even raising her voice, she laid out the deal—either you leave and never see your daughter, the house, or her again, or you stay. If you chose to stay, you were in charge of finding a counselor and working it out. Was it weird that you found that completely arousing? Obviously, you chose to stay and seek help for your indiscretions.

You never asked how she found out, even years later when you were sure she had moved past it. It never seemed the right thing to ask. For all you knew, it may have been a wild guess which you promptly confirmed. Truth be told, you have always been intimidated by your wife and have always known better than to deny any misdeeds to her. She is too smart for that. You lied to the gal at the clinic, insisting you were single, but she didn't deserve the truth; she didn't deserve your honesty. Your wife, though, demands it.

The one big mistake people often make is thinking your wife is some dumb, dutiful housewife. You quickly learned she's smart as a whip. The first time you realized this you were in the kitchen making yourself a sandwich because you came home late without letting her know, and she threw your dinner in the trash. You'd only been married for a year or two, tops. You peered in the trash and saw roasted chicken, green beans, and some noodle concoction. For a split second, you considered retrieving it, but you knew this would only make you look pathetic in her eyes. And that was the last thing you wanted.

She was watching Jeopardy in the living room, and lo and behold, she knew almost every answer. You peered into the room and saw she was reading a book while doing this. This was when you realized she was either the best or worst decision you had ever made in your life.

She came from nothing. Her parents died in a car accident when she was young, and she and her two older siblings were raised by their grandparents, who did the best they could with the little they had, which was damn well near to nothing.

Her grandfather had worked in the coal mines of Kentucky. And soon enough his lungs gave out, and he too passed away. Her grandmother slowly lost all sense of everything. Dementia, they called it. So, her older brother took over the household. How she ended up at the university's library was a feat and a miracle all on its own.

Sometimes you rummage through the shoebox pushed to the back of her closet. It is mixed in with other shoeboxes, but it's the oldest, most tattered one of the bunch, its brand now unrecognizable. This is the only thing left of her past. It's filled with yellowed birthday cards, postcards, and letters from relatives and other less identifiable people from her past, faded black and white photographs of stern, gaunt faces, a diary written in a child's handwriting, and most surprisingly, a baseball card of Sandy Koufax protected by a thick plastic sleeve. Every time you open it, you expect there to be a timeline jotted down in the pages of the diary, outlining how to get out and move up in the world. Because once she reeled you in, she got pregnant and stopped working. She went from a librarian eating dinner out of cans to the wife of a prominent dentist. Gumption, that's what she's got.

You rush into the house, ditching your tie and khakis on the unmade bed and slipping into your camouflage. As you leave with shotgun in hand, you grab the turkey calls from the refrigerator. You know you are better than most when it comes to evoking the proper hen call using these refrigerated mouthpieces. You're like a siren to gobblers, luring them straight for the wrong end of an aimed barrel. You know it's an art. Your buddies are always asking you for advice. "What can I say, other than that I'm good with my mouth," you tell them. They always laugh.

You already know where you're going to hunt. You heard some turkeys mucking about along the power line this morning on your run. As a last-minute impulse, you grab a turkey decoy. You walk, instead of riding the four-wheeler, through your family's land. Your house sits on 200 acres, all your family's property. You and your brother share a hundred while an uncle owns the other half. All the hunting stands and areas are designated numerically on an enlarged aerial shot of the property. Everyone who hunts, which is mostly family and the occasional invited friend, must sign in where they are hunting using the map.

You set up shop at #21, placing the decoy a good 10 yards away and off to the right from where you perch against a tree at the edge of the opening. You like the power-line's view, open and endless to the naked eye. You can hear the cars on the country roads screeching to a halt at the stop sign in front of Donna's One Stop, with the catchy motto: "Stop one time and never go back." You made this up, and when you told your wife, she laughed harder than you ever thought possible. She wasn't a big fan of Donna, with her big, bleached-blonde hair, chili-stained tank tops, and jean shorts that cut into her dented thighs.

You begin your serenading call, sweet music to a gobbler's senses. Suddenly, you hear a gobbler calling back. Your calls become more insistent and eager when you realize the gobbler is not alone but is in the company of a female companion. You, the gobbler, and his hen begin an incessant conversation, with you and the hen fighting for the attention of the lone gobbler. Just when you think you've been defeated, you see the gobbler rushing full speed ahead towards the decoy hen set up. You aim. You shoot. You kill.

The old boy has a 9-inch beard. He's a beauty—a poor, pathetic beauty. This is what you will tell your buddies around the table at 521 Grill, where you have eaten lunch almost every day for the last 25 years. You will tell them the story and the irony of the gobbler's demise. You will tell them how after you killed him, you bent down and whispered, "Should have stuck by the one you're with."

You won't tell them how the breeze rustled through the pines, forcing you to look up at the flushed sky and wonder if this could be a metaphor for life. You also won't reveal how the high from the kill and the view of the burnt sun sinking into green earth made you profess aloud, "Yes, I know."

What do you know? The truth. The truth that marriage is hard, if not impossible for many, and it rarely makes an honest man out of anyone. The other truth is you wouldn't trade it for the world and definitely not for a deadly blow to the chest. Yes, you wonder what it would be like to sleep with someone else or heck, just someone new. But this you know to be a fleeting feeling. And sure women say trust is the sexiest thing on a man, and you would say, if asked and if honest, that confidence is the sexiest thing on a woman— not confidence in herself but confidence in you.

You often think about Aunt Millie and her thankfulness for her husband being dead. But if you read into it, it could really mean so many things. Then again, you remember Harold was a five-star asshole—mean-spirited with a quick temper that could turn into honey on a dime. No wonder she cursed like an angry, plotting sailor.

"There I stood, squirtin' like a goose," you think to yourself and smile as you pluck a feather off the gobbler's peaceful carcass and stick it in your cap—proof of the kill, proof it was real.

LANCE NIZAMI has no formal training in the Arts. He is active in the world's most competitive profession, yet without an institutional appointment. He started writing poetry during a long airplane flight in late 2010, and has written much since then in-flight. As of 3 April 2015 he had 155 poems in print or in press (not online), the most recent acceptances being at *Paper and Ink Literary Zine*, *Edwin E. Smith's Quarterly Magazine*, and *The Transnational*.

Enlightenment

The budding bodhisattva sits in front of his computer
Inwardly, he sees a rocky hilltop in the Himalayas
There, a string of prayer flags is wildly flapping, strung
between rock cairns

The bodhisattva wishes he were there, in Buddha's country
Except that it was never Buddha's country; Buddha
preached in verdant valleys
The Buddha sat beneath a tree, not high upon the hilltop in
the cold

The hilltop is for hermits and for hunters and for
Himalayan tahrs
The hilltop is for foolish bodhisattvas who think altitude is
grace
A bodhisattva thinks that higher heights will lead to deeper
insights there

Perspective geography gives perspective of the mind, or so
he thinks
But no; he'll find enlightenment cross-legged under trees –
He'll find the people there, the ones whose ancestors heard
Buddha

Those ancestors, like bodhisattva, thought the hilltops holy,
but were wrong
The holy place was underneath the tree, where they gained
strength from hearing Buddha
The holy place was underneath the tree.

Mind and Matter

There was a time that I could read her mind
But did it matter?

Sure it did
It meant, at times, that I could make things matter all the
better

And did she like that? Sure, but matters more important
would intrude
And I could not move matter with my mind—

Telepathic, yes, but not kinetic, merely empathetic
And soon, affairs dramatic interrupted matters automatic

Minding my own feelings, I soon stepped aside, let feelings
take their course
A mighty flow of feelings took a nightly course meandering

And did I mind? Meanders introduced the things that
mattered, in her thoughts—
Was I among them? I could only hope that I was featured—

There was a time that I could read her mind
But did it matter?

BEAU BOUDREAUX teaches English in Continuing Studies at Tulane University in New Orleans. His first book-length collection of poetry, *Running Redder, Running Redder*, was published in the spring of 2012 by Cherry Grove Collections. His poetry appears in *Antioch Review*, *Cream City Review*, and *The Southern Poetry Anthology*.

After Dinner

Pleasure comes from
taking out the trash

on Monday and Thursday night
from the kitchen can

I cinch up the bag
heavy—knot the strings

waltz out to the green bin
snug on the curb.

If I'm lucky, my wife brings out
a fresh bag of Glad

lines the can for tomorrow.

Attic

Came early on my list to order and purge
two laptops from another century

and a working monitor—recycle at Best Buy.
Plastic bins with Christmas ornaments

and photo albums easy to stack on the right wall.
Some fifty stock wine glasses

black and white Rolling Stones posters—
Ebay candidates, along with framed floral prints.

But the dissertation notes wearing
leather cases, Iowa workshop folders

much less letters from Medbh in Belfast
and the collar from my first beagle...

at least there are two clear paths on the floorboards
along the heating units, a clean promise for spring.